WORSHIP
THE LORD

edited by

James R. Esther
Donald J. Bruggink

1987
THE REFORMED CHURCH IN AMERICA

WM. B. EERDMANS PUBLISHING COMPANY

Copyright © 1987 by The Reformed Church in America
475 Riverside Drive, New York, New York 10115

Prepared by the Commission on Worship of the Reformed Church in America
Design and layout by Joel Beversluis
Text type: Goudy Old Style
Printed and bound by Eerdmans Printing Company, Grand Rapids, Michigan

Library of Congress Cataloging-in-Publication Data

Worship the Lord.

"Prepared by the Commission on Worship of the Reformed
Church in America"—T.p. verso.
1. Reformed Church in America—Liturgy—Texts.
2. Reformed Church—Liturgy—Texts. I. Esther, James R., 1941-   .
II. Bruggink, Donald J. III. Reformed Church in America. Commission on Worship.
BX9523.W67 1987   264'.57   87-9299

ISBN 0-8028-0330-X

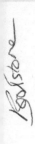

CONTENTS

Those of the Reformed Church in America who have served on its Worship Commission from 1976 to 1986 when these liturgical forms and the directory in this volume were developed were:

Stuart J. Blauw, 1976-82
Randall B. Bosch, 1974-77
Donald J. Bruggink, 1980-86
Robert J. DeYoung, 1985—
Gordon R. Dragt, 1972-77
James R. Esther, 1973-86 (Moderator, 1980-86)
Betty Garee, 1979-80
Kenneth A. Gorsuch, 1977-84
Howard G. Hageman, 1973-78 (Moderator, 1973-78)
Harold Leestma, 1978-80
Louis Lotz, 1984-87
Gregg Mast, 1982-85
Melody Meeter, 1984—
Carol Myers, 1981— (Moderator, 1986—)
A. Eugene Pearson, 1973-79
Roger J. Rietberg, 1974-80
Arlen R. Salthouse, 1974-80 (Moderator, 1978-80)
Thomas F. Schwanda, 1978-1984
Mary Van Andel, 1983—
Lawrence Van Wyk, 1977-83

Also to be recognized for their contributions are:

Eugene P. Heideman
Nancy Van Wyk Phillips

INTRODUCTION

Worship the Lord offers liturgical forms for public worship in congregations and classes. The use of the Order of Worship which contains the Sacrament of the Lord's Supper, the Orders for the Sacrament of Baptism, Reception into Communicant Membership, the Ordination and Installation of Elders and Deacons, and the Installation of a Minister or Missionary have been approved by the General Synod and classes as supplemental to those in the *Liturgy and Psalms.*

The Orders for Marriage, Healing, and Burial have been approved by the General Synod and commended to the churches.

Worship the Lord also contains the *Directory for Worship.* The General Synod of 1986 adopted the *Directory* as a "constituent part of the RCA *Constitution*, equal in authority to the *Liturgy* of the RCA" for recommendation to the classes for approval. The *Directory* defines standards for the nature, content, and order of Christian worship.

Our Song of Hope was approved by the General Synod of 1978 as a statement of the church's faith for use in its ministry of witness, teaching, and worship. In the liturgy, it is to be used as a confession of faith. *Our Song of Hope* has been placed at the end of *Worship the Lord* for easy access in congregational worship.

The Commission on Worship

James R. Esther
Donald J. Bruggink
Editors

PART I
Congregational Services

ORDER OF WORSHIP

The service of worship ordinarily begins with the Votum, Sentences, and Salutation.
Or it may begin with the Hymn, especially if it is a processional, followed by the
Votum, Sentences, and Salutation. The portions printed in bold type are intended
to be read by the congregation.

THE APPROACH TO GOD

VOTUM

Our help is in the name of the Lord, who made heaven and earth. **Amen.**

Psalm 124:8

SENTENCES

The following, or other appropriate portions of Scripture, may be used.

O come, let us worship and bow down, let us kneel before the Lord, our Maker!
For he is our God, and we are the people of his pasture, and the sheep of his
hand. *Psalm 95:6-7*

and/or

Psalm 33:1-5	*Psalm 100*	*Zechariah 8:7-8*
Psalm 43:3-4	*Exodus 15:2*	*John 4:24*
Psalm 96:1-3	*Isaiah 55:1, 6-7*	

SALUTATION

Grace to you and peace from God our Father and the Lord Jesus Christ. **Amen.**

or

Galatians 1:3-5	*II Peter 1:2*	*Jude 2*
I Timothy 1:2	*II John 3*	*Revelation 1:4-5*
Titus 1:4		

HYMN

PRAYER OF CONFESSION

The minister may introduce the prayer with the following or another suitable call
to confession.

Let us confess our sins to almighty God. Let us pray.

All shall join in one of the following prayers or another appropriate confession.

Have mercy upon us, O God, according to your steadfast love; according to
your abundant mercies, blot out our transgressions. Wash us thoroughly
from our iniquity, and cleanse us from our sin. For we know our transgres-
sions, and our sin is ever before us. Create in us a clean heart, O God, and
put a new and right spirit within us. Cast us not away from your presence,
and take not your Holy Spirit from us. Restore to us the joy of your sal-
vation, and uphold us with a willing spirit. Through Jesus Christ our Lord.
Amen. *Adapted from Psalm 51*

or

Most holy and merciful Father, we acknowledge and confess before you our sinful nature, prone to evil and slow to do good; and all our shortcomings and offenses. You alone know how often we have sinned: in wandering from your ways, in wasting your gifts, in forgetting your love. But, O Lord, have mercy on us, who are ashamed and sorry for all wherein we have displeased you. Teach us to hate our errors; cleanse us from our secret faults; and forgive our sins; for the sake of your dear Son. And, O most holy and loving God, help us to live in your light and walk in your ways, according to the commandments of Jesus Christ, our Savior. Amen.

A brief period for silent prayers may be allowed. The following or another suitable response may then be said or sung (see Rejoice in the Lord [henceforth: RIL], 564-567):

Lord, have mercy upon us.
Christ, have mercy upon us.
Lord, have mercy upon us.

ASSURANCE OF PARDON

One of the following scriptural assurances or one drawn from other portions of Scripture may be used to convey an assurance of God's promise freely to pardon all who come to him in repentance and faith.

The LORD is merciful and gracious, slow to anger and abounding in steadfast love. He does not deal with us according to our sins, nor requite us according to our iniquities. For as the heavens are high above the earth, so great is his steadfast love toward those who fear him; as far as the east is from the west, so far does he remove our transgressions from us.   *Psalm 103:8, 10-12*

or

With everlasting love I will have compassion on you, says the LORD your Redeemer. I, I am he who blots out your transgressions for my own sake, and I will not remember your sins. Return to me, for I have redeemed you.   *Isaiah 54:8; 43:25; 44:22*

or

Can a woman forget her sucking child, that she have no compassion on the child of her womb? As a mother comforts her child, so will I comfort you, says the LORD.   *Isaiah 49:15; 66:13*

or

For God so loved the world that he gave his only Son, that whoever believes in him should not perish, but have eternal life. For God sent the Son into the world, not to condemn the world, but that the world might be saved through him.   *John 3:16-17*

or

Psalm 130:3-4, 7	*Isaiah 44:21-22*	*John 8:34-36*
Psalm 145:18-19	*Luke 1:68, 77-78*	*Colossians 1:11-14*

At the conclusion of the scriptural assurance, the minister shall add:

Believe this Gospel and go forth to live in peace. **Amen.**

THE LAW OF GOD

The Law may be read or sung, or the service may proceed to the reading of the Summary. To sing a metrical version of the law use RIL, hymn 65.

God spoke all these words, saying, I am the LORD your God who brought you out of the land of Egypt, out of the house of bondage.

You shall have no other gods before me.

You shall not make yourself a graven image, *or any likeness of anything that is in the heaven above, or that is in the earth beneath, or that is in the water under the earth; you shall not bow down to them or serve them; for I the LORD your God am a jealous God, visiting the iniquity of the fathers upon the children to the third and fourth generation of those who hate me, but showing steadfast love to thousands of those who love me and keep my commandments.*

You shall not take the name of the LORD your God in vain; *for the LORD will not hold him guiltless who takes his name in vain.*

Remember the sabbath day, to keep it holy. *Six days you shall labor, and do all your work; but the seventh day is the sabbath to the LORD your God; in it you shall not do any work, you, or your son, or your daughter, your manservant, or your maidservant, or your cattle, or the sojourner who is within your gates; for in six days the LORD made heaven and earth, the sea, and all that is in them, and rested the seventh day; therefore the LORD blessed the sabbath day and hallowed it.*

Honor your father and your mother, *that your days may be long in the land which the LORD your God gives you.*

You shall not kill.

You shall not commit adultery.

You shall not steal.

You shall not bear false witness *against your neighbor.*

You shall not covet *your neighbor's house; you shall not covet your neighbor's wife, or his manservant, or his maidservant, or his ox, or his ass, or anything that is your neighbor's.*   *Exodus 20:1-17*

    and/or

Hear what our Lord Jesus Christ says:

You shall love the Lord your God with all your heart, and with all your soul, and with all your mind. This is the great and first commandment. And a second is like it, you shall love your neighbor as yourself. On these two commandments depend all the law and the prophets.   *Matthew 22:37-40*

    or as it is recorded in Mark 12:29-31.

PSALTER AND GLORIA PATRI

A selection from the Psalms and the Gloria Patri or another appropriate hymn may be used to express gratitude to God.

THE WORD OF GOD
IN PROCLAMATION AND SACRAMENT

PRAYER FOR ILLUMINATION

This prayer or another petition may be offered.

Guide us, O Lord, by your Word and Holy Spirit, that in your light we may see light, in your truth find freedom, and in your will discover peace; through Jesus Christ our Lord. **Amen.**

HYMN

A hymn setting forth the theme of the Scripture reading(s) or praising God for the revelation in his Word may be sung here, between the lessons, or before the sermon.

LESSONS

There will ordinarily be two or three lessons, one from the Old Testament, one from the portion of the New Testament other than the Gospels, and one from the Gospels. The lessons may be announced as follows:

The Word of the Lord from _____

After the reading of the lesson there may be the response.

This is the Word of the Lord.

Thanks be to God.

The Gospel may be announced as follows:

The Gospel of our Lord Jesus Christ according to _____

The following may be used as a response to the Gospel.

This is the Gospel of the Lord.

Praise to you, O Christ.

SERMON

The minister shall deliver a sermon proclaiming the Scripture of the day.

PRAYER FOR BLESSING

Almighty God, grant that the words we have heard this day may, through your grace, be so grafted within our hearts that they may bring forth in us the fruits of the Spirit, to the honor and praise of your name; through Jesus Christ our Lord. **Amen.**

The minister shall move to the table.

When worship includes only the grace of the WORD IN PROCLAMATION, then the Creed, Offering, Doxology, Prayers of Thanksgiving and Intercession, Hymn, and Benediction may be understood as the congregation's RESPONSE TO GOD.

CONFESSION OF FAITH

The minister shall call the people to join in an affirmation of the Christian faith.

Let us confess our Christian faith using the Nicene [*or* Apostles' (see p. 8)] Creed:

When all have risen, the minister shall say:

Let us say what we believe.

I. THE NICENE CREED

We believe in one God,
the Father, the Almighty,
maker of heaven and earth,
of all that is, seen and unseen.

We believe in one Lord, Jesus Christ,
the only Son of God,
eternally begotten of the Father,
God from God, Light from Light,
true God from true God,
begotten, not made,
of one being with the Father.
Through him all things were made.
For us and for our salvation
he came down from heaven:
by the power of the Holy Spirit
he became incarnate from the virgin Mary,
and was made man.
For our sake he was crucified under Pontius Pilate;
he suffered death and was buried.
On the third day he rose again
in accordance with the Scriptures;
he ascended into heaven
and is seated at the right hand of the Father.
He will come again in glory to judge the living and the dead,
and his kingdom will have no end.

We believe in the Holy Spirit, the Lord, the giver of life,
who proceeds from the Father and the Son.
With the Father and the Son he is worshiped and glorified.
He has spoken through the Prophets.
We believe in one holy catholic and apostolic Church.
We acknowledge one baptism for the forgiveness of sins.
We look for the resurrection of the dead,
and the life of the world to come. Amen.

or

II. THE NICENE CREED

We believe in one God,
   the Father almighty,
   maker of heaven and earth,
   and of all things visible and invisible;

And in one Lord Jesus Christ,
   the only-begotten Son of God,
   begotten of his Father before all worlds,
   God of God, Light of Light,
   very God of very God,
   begotten, not made,
   being of one substance with the Father;
   by whom all things were made;
   who for us and for our salvation
      came down from heaven,
   and was incarnate by the Holy Ghost of the Virgin Mary,
      and was made man;
   and was crucified also for us under Pontius Pilate;
   he suffered and was buried;
   and the third day he rose again according to the Scriptures,
   and ascended into heaven,
   and sitteth on the right hand of the Father;
   and he shall come again, with glory,
      to judge both the quick and the dead;
   whose kingdom shall have no end.

And we believe in the Holy Ghost, the Lord and giver of life,
   who proceedeth from the Father and the Son;
   who with the Father and the Son together is worshiped
      and glorified;
   who spake by the Prophets.
   and we believe one holy catholic and apostolic Church;
   we acknowledge one baptism for the remission of sins;
   and we look for the resurrection of the dead,
      and the life of the world to come. Amen.

or

I. THE APOSTLES' CREED

I believe in God, the Father almighty,
  creator of heaven and earth.

I believe in Jesus Christ, his only Son, our Lord.
  He was conceived by the power of the Holy Spirit
    and born of the Virgin Mary.
  He suffered under Pontius Pilate,
    was crucified, died, and was buried.
  He descended to the dead.
  On the third day he rose again.
  He ascended into heaven,
    and is seated at the right hand of the Father.
  He will come again to judge the living and the dead.

I believe in the Holy Spirit,
  the holy catholic Church,
  the communion of saints,
  the forgiveness of sins,
  the resurrection of the body,
  and the life everlasting. Amen.

or

II. THE APOSTLES' CREED

I believe in God, the Father almighty,
  maker of heaven and earth;

And in Jesus Christ, his only Son, our Lord;
  who was conceived by the Holy Ghost,
  born of the Virgin Mary,
  suffered under Pontius Pilate,
  was crucified, dead, and buried.
  He descended into hell.
  The third day he rose again from the dead.
  He ascended into heaven,
  and sitteth on the right hand of God the Father almighty.
  From thence he shall come to judge the quick and the dead.

I believe in the Holy Ghost,
  the holy catholic Church,
  the communion of saints,
  the forgiveness of sins,
  the resurrection of the body,
  and the life everlasting. Amen.

N.B. A metrical version of the creed may be sung using RIL, hymn 609.

PEACE

The minister may introduce the Peace with these, or other appropriate words of Scripture:

Let the peace of Christ rule in your hearts since as members of one body you were called to peace.   *Colossians 3:15*

The peace of Christ be with you.

And also with you.

The congregation may then exchange the Peace using the same greeting and response or through other appropriate words and actions.

OFFERING

An offering shall be received to provide for a ministry within the congregation, to gather resources for the ministries of others, and to provide the elements for the celebration of the Lord's Supper.

DOXOLOGY

This hymn, or another ascription of praise, may be used as the offerings are brought forward.

MEANING OF THE SACRAMENT

Beloved in the Lord Jesus Christ, the holy Supper which we are about to celebrate is a feast of remembrance, of communion, and of hope.

We come in remembrance that our Lord Jesus Christ was sent of the Father into the world to assume our flesh and blood and to fulfil for us all obedience to the divine law, even to the bitter and shameful death of the cross. By his death, resurrection, and ascension he established a new and eternal covenant of grace and reconciliation that we might be accepted of God and never be forsaken by him.

We come to have communion with this same Christ who has promised to be with us always, even to the end of the world. In the breaking of the bread he makes himself known to us as the true heavenly Bread that strengthens us unto life eternal. In the cup of blessing he comes to us as the Vine in whom we must abide if we are to bear fruit.

We come in hope, believing that this bread and this cup are a pledge and foretaste of the feast of love of which we shall partake when his kingdom has fully come, when with unveiled face we shall behold him, made like unto him in his glory.

Since by his death, resurrection, and ascension Christ has obtained for us the life-giving Spirit who unites us all in one body, so are we to receive this Supper in true love, mindful of the communion of saints.

INVITATION

The minister, in the name of Christ, shall extend an invitation to all communicants present to participate in the Sacrament. The following, or a similar invitation, may be said.

All those who have confessed their faith in Christ and are members of a Christian church are welcome at the Lord's Table. Come, for all things are now ready.

COMMUNION PRAYER

The Lord be with you.

And also with you.

Lift up your hearts!

We lift them up to the Lord.

Let us give thanks to the Lord our God.

For it is holy and right to do so!

Holy and right it is, and our joyful duty to give thanks to you at all times and in all places, O Lord our Creator, almighty and everlasting God! You created heaven with all its hosts and the earth with all its plenty. You have given us life and being, and preserve us by your providence. But you have shown us the fullness of your love in sending into the world your Son, Jesus Christ, the eternal Word, made flesh for us and for our salvation. For the precious gift of this mighty Savior who has reconciled us to you we praise and bless you, O God. With your whole Church on earth and with all the company of heaven we worship and adore your glorious name.

Here all shall say or sing (where sung see RIL, hymns 564-567):

Holy, holy, holy, Lord God of hosts! Heaven and earth are full of your glory. Hosanna in the highest!

Blessed is he that comes in the name of the Lord. Hosanna in the highest!

A short period of silence

Most righteous God, we remember in this Supper the perfect sacrifice offered once on the cross by our Lord Jesus Christ for the sin of the whole world.

In the joy of his resurrection and in expectation of his coming again, we offer ourselves to you as holy and living sacrifices. Send your Holy Spirit upon us, we pray, that the bread which we break and the cup which we bless may be to us the communion of the body and blood of Christ. Grant that, being joined together in him, we may attain to the unity of the faith and grow up in all things into Christ our Lord.

And as this grain has been gathered from many fields into one loaf, and these grapes from many hills into one cup, grant, O Lord, that your whole Church may soon be gathered from the ends of the earth into your kingdom. Even so, come, Lord Jesus!

COMMUNION

The minister shall declare the Words of Institution:

The Lord Jesus, the same night he was betrayed, took bread; and when he had given thanks, he broke it and gave it to them, saying, "Take, eat; this is my body which is broken for you: do this in remembrance of me."

The minister shall break the bread.

After the same manner also, he took the cup when they had supped, saying, "This cup is the new testament in my blood: this do, as often as you drink it, in remembrance of me."

The minister shall lift the cup.

The bread which we break is the communion of the body of Christ.

The cup of blessing which we bless is the communion of the blood of Christ.

THE RESPONSE TO GOD

THANKSGIVING AFTER COMMUNION

Brothers and sisters, since the Lord has now fed us at his Table, let us praise God's holy name with heartfelt thanksgiving!

Bless the LORD, O my soul;

and all that is within me, bless his holy name!

Bless the LORD, O my soul,

and forget not all his benefits,

who forgives all your iniquity,

who heals all your diseases,

who redeems your life from the Pit,

who crowns you with steadfast love and mercy.

The LORD is merciful and gracious,

slow to anger and abounding in steadfast love.

He does not deal with us according to our sins,

nor requite us according to our iniquities.

For as the heavens are high above the earth,

so great is his steadfast love toward those who fear him;

as far as the east is from the west,

so far does he remove our transgressions from us.

As a father pities his children,

so the LORD pities those who fear him.

Who did not spare his own Son, but gave him up for us all, and will also give us all things with him.

Therefore shall my mouth and heart show forth the praise of the Lord, from this time forth forevermore. Amen.   *From Psalm 103 with additions*

N.B. This thanksgiving can be sung using RIL, hymn 121, 122, or 144.

INTERCESSION

The following prayers may be used. Intercessions may be selected from other sources or may be in the minister's own words. The intercessions shall conclude with the Lord's Prayer.

Let us pray.

We praise and thank you, O Lord, that you have fed us at your Table. Grateful for your gifts and mindful of the communion of your saints, we offer to you our prayers for all people.

God of compassion, we remember before you the poor and the afflicted, the sick and the dying, prisoners and all who are lonely, the victims of war, injustice, and inhumanity, and all others who suffer from whatever their sufferings may be called.

Silence

O Lord of Providence, who holds the destiny of the nations in your hand, we pray for our country. Inspire the hearts and minds of our leaders that they, together with all our nation, may first seek your kingdom and righteousness so that order, liberty, and peace may dwell with your people.

Silence

O God the Creator, we pray for all nations and peoples. Take away the mistrust and lack of understanding that divide your creatures; increase in us the recognition that we are all your children.

Silence

O Savior God, look upon your Church in its struggle upon the earth. Have mercy on its weakness, bring to an end its unhappy divisions, and scatter its fears. Look also upon the ministry of your Church. Increase its courage, strengthen its faith, and inspire its witness to all people, even to the ends of the earth.

Silence

Author of grace and God of love, send your Holy Spirit's blessing to your children here present. Keep our hearts and thoughts in Jesus Christ, your Son, our only Savior

who has taught us to pray:	*or*	who has taught us when we pray to say:
Our Father in heaven, 　**hallowed be your name,** 　**your kingdom come,** 　**your will be done,** 　　**on earth as in heaven.** **Give us today our daily bread.** **Forgive us our sins** 　**as we forgive those** 　　**who sin against us.** **Save us from the time of trial,** 　**and deliver us from evil.** **For the kingdom, the power,** 　**and the glory are yours,** **now and for ever. Amen.**		**Our Father, who art in heaven,** 　**hallowed be thy name,** 　**thy kingdom come,** 　**thy will be done,** 　　**on earth as it is in heaven.** **Give us this day our daily bread.** **And forgive us our debts,** 　**as we forgive our debtors.** **And lead us not into temptation,** 　**but deliver us from evil.** **For thine is the kingdom,** 　**and the power, and the glory,** 　**for ever. Amen.**

NB.: *The Lord's Prayer may be sung using RIL, hymn 262.*

HYMN　　*A hymn or psalm of thanksgiving may be sung.*

BENEDICTION　*Facing the congregation, the minister shall give the blessing:*

The grace of the Lord Jesus Christ and the love of God and the fellowship of the Holy Spirit be with you all. **Amen!**　　　　*II Corinthians 13:14*

or

Numbers 6:24-26	*Luke 2:29-32*	*II Thessalonians 3:16*
Psalm 67:1-2	*Romans 15:5-6*	*Hebrews 13:20-21*

THE SACRAMENT OF BAPTISM

The Sacrament of Baptism should be administered on the Lord's Day during the primary service of worship. The requirements of the Reformed Church in America regarding the sacrament should have been met fully before the administration of baptism takes place.

Baptism shall be administered using water, by sprinkling, pouring, or immersion. It shall take place before the whole congregation.

MEANING OF THE SACRAMENT

The continuity of the Meaning is maintained in the paragraphs in roman type. The paragraphs in italics may be selected to set forth the doctrine in greater fullness.

Beloved in the Lord, the Sacrament of Baptism is a visible, holy sign and seal instituted by God so that he may the more fully reveal and seal to us the promise of the gospel, that because of the one sacrifice of Christ on the cross we are, through grace alone, granted the forgiveness of our sins and given new and eternal life.

In baptism God reveals and seals to us his mercy and forgiveness. For, though we are sinners, sinful in our very nature, our sins are washed away in Christ's blood, poured out for us on the cross, and our old, sinful nature is crucified with him so that we might be brought to live new and holy lives. Of this the Apostle Paul reminds us:

Do you not know that all of us who have been baptized into Christ Jesus were baptized into his death? We were buried therefore with him by baptism into death, so that as Christ was raised from the dead by the glory of the Father, we too might walk in newness of life. Romans 6:3-4

In baptism God reveals and seals to us his covenant of salvation, given first to Noah and his whole family whom God saved from the waters of the flood, and renewed time after time through the Patriarchs and Prophets until it reached perfection in the person of Jesus Christ our Lord. We participate in this covenant through faith in Christ, and in him become a new creation. So Scripture promises through the Gospel writer John:

To all who receive him, to those who believed in his name, he gave the right to become children of God—children born not of natural descent, nor of human decision or a husband's will, but born of God. John 1:12-13 NIV

In baptism God reveals and seals to us the sanctifying power of the Holy Spirit who through the sacrament assures us that our whole salvation is rooted in the one sacrifice of Christ on the cross. Through the Holy Spirit God begins this good work in us and daily renews us, setting us apart to be members of Christ so that more and more we may die to sin and live in a consecrated and blameless way. So the Apostle Paul speaks to us:

When the kindness and love of God our Savior appeared, he saved us, not because of righteous things we had done, but because of his mercy. He saved us through the washing of rebirth and renewal by the Holy Spirit, whom he poured out on us generously through Jesus Christ our Savior, so that, having been justified by his grace, we might become heirs having the hope of eternal life. Titus 3:4-7 NIV

The sign and seal of this promise is made visible in the water of baptism, for as surely as water cleanses us physically, so surely does the blood of Christ cleanse us spiritually.

The promise is for you and your children and for all who are far off—for all whom the Lord our God will call.   *Acts 2:39 NIV*

INSTITUTION

After his resurrection the Lord Jesus came to his disciples and said:

All authority in heaven and on earth has been given to me. Go therefore and make disciples of all nations, baptizing them in the name of the Father and of the Son and of the Holy Spirit, teaching them to observe all that I have commanded you; and lo, I am with you always, to the close of the age.
Matthew 28:18-20

VOWS

It is in fulfillment of our Lord's institution and command
that the Church now administers holy baptism to

N. _____   *(full names)*
I ask   *him*   *her*   *them*
      and   *his*   *her*   *their parents*
to come before the congregation now
that we may together affirm our faith,
renew our commitment,
and ask God for his grace.

      When they have taken their place before the font, the minister shall say:

Let us stand together.

      Then, addressing the candidate(s) or the parents, the minister shall continue:

Beloved in the Lord, you stand before us
      having brought   *this child*   *these children*
to receive the Sacrament of Baptism.
Therefore, before God and Christ's Church I ask
you to answer sincerely these questions:

Do you accept the Gospel of God's grace in Jesus Christ revealed in the holy Scripture of the Old and New Testaments as the only way to eternal life?

I do.

Do you acknowledge that you
      and   *this child*   *these children*
are *(a)* sinner(s), sinful by nature, but that by the grace of God alone your sins are forgiven and your old nature is put to death, so that you may be brought to newness of life and set apart as *a* member(s) of the body of Christ?

I do.

Do you promise to pray
      for your   *child*   *children,*
for yourself, and for others, asking God's guidance
      in training   *him*   *her*   *them*

as together we seek to grow in knowledge
and understanding of the faith?

I do.

Do you promise to show in your own person the joy of new life in Christ;
by active participation
   with him her them
in the life of the Church and by faithful attendance to worship, service,
and the offering of prayers and gifts, to the glory of God?

**I do, and I ask God, and you his people, to help me to keep these
promises.**

   When all have risen, the minister shall address the congregation.

Do you the members of this congregation now renew your own baptismal
vows as you celebrate this sacrament of grace?

We do.

Do you promise to seek God's guidance as you welcome
   this these brother(s) and sister(s)
into the community of faith and as you provide
   him her them
with Christian love and nurture through your prayers and encouragement,
your teaching and affection?

We do.

Let us confess our Christian faith using the Apostles' Creed:

I. THE APOSTLES' CREED

I believe in God, the Father almighty,
 creator of heaven and earth.

I believe in Jesus Christ, his only Son, our Lord.
 He was conceived by the power of the Holy Spirit
  and born of the Virgin Mary.
 He suffered under Pontius Pilate,
  was crucified, died, and was buried.
 He descended to the dead.
 On the third day he rose again.
 He ascended into heaven,
  and is seated at the right hand of the Father.
 He will come again to judge the living and the dead.

I believe in the Holy Spirit,
 the holy catholic Church,
 the communion of saints,
 the forgiveness of sins,
 the resurrection of the body,
 and the life everlasting. Amen.

II. THE APOSTLES' CREED

I believe in God, the Father almighty,
    maker of heaven and earth;

And in Jesus Christ, his only Son, our Lord;
    who was conceived by the Holy Ghost,
    born of the Virgin Mary,
    suffered under Pontius Pilate,
    was crucified, dead, and buried.
    He descended into hell.
    The third day he rose again from the dead.
    He ascended into heaven,
    and sitteth on the right hand of God the Father almighty.
    From thence he shall come to judge the quick and the dead.

I believe in the Holy Ghost,
    the holy catholic Church,
    the communion of saints,
    the forgiveness of sins,
    the resurrection of the body,
    and the life everlasting. Amen.

> *N.B. A metrical version of the creed may be sung using RIL, hymn 609.*

> *The congregation may be seated. If it has not already been done, the minister may pour water into the font.*

PRAYER

Let us pray.

Almighty God, we thank you for Jesus Christ, who by his sacrifice of death on the cross has saved us from our sin, and by his resurrection from the dead has given us the blessing of eternal life. We praise you that, in Christ, you have made a covenant of grace with your people and appointed the holy Sacrament of Baptism to be its sign and seal.

Send your Holy Spirit to us now, that we who celebrate this sacrament may be renewed in our participation in the saving work of Christ, and that
    this your child   these your children.
who now receive(s) the water of baptism may also receive spiritual cleansing and newness of life through the Holy Spirit's power. And remembering that we are not our own, but belong—body and soul, in life and in death—to our faithful Savior Jesus Christ, we offer ourselves to you, asking you to work in us that which is pleasing in your sight, through the same Jesus Christ our Lord. **Amen.**

ADMINISTRATION OF THE SACRAMENT

> *If there are infants or small children to be baptized the minister may hold them to administer the sacrament. Others to be baptized shall kneel. The minister shall baptize each with water saying:*

I baptize you in the name of the Father and of the Son and of the Holy Spirit. **Amen.**

The following declaration may be made:

In the name of the Lord Jesus Christ, the only King and Head of his Church, I declare that this child is now received into the visible membership of the Holy Catholic Church, and is engaged to confess the faith of Christ crucified, and to be his faithful servant unto   *his   her*   life's end.

or this at the baptism of adults:

This child of God is received into the Body of Christ, the Holy Catholic Church. "The Spirit himself testifies with our spirit that we are God's children. Now if we are children, then we are heirs—heirs of God and coheirs with Christ, if indeed we share in his sufferings in order that we may also share in his glory."   *Romans 8:16-17 NIV*

After baptism has been administered, the following prayer shall be offered:

PRAYER

Let us pray.
O Lord, through your grace alone you cleanse and renew
this your child   these your children.
Bless   *him   her   them*
and strengthen   *him   her   them*   daily
with the power of the Holy Spirit;
unfold to   *him   her   them,*
more and more,
the riches of your love
and deepen   *his   her   their*   faith;
keep   *him   her   them*   from the power of evil,
enabling   *him   her   them*   to live
a holy and blameless life until your kingdom comes.

At the baptism of infants

Bless your servants, these parents, that they may keep the promises they have made. Grant them your presence and your Holy Spirit that they may bring up their   *child   children*   to know you, love you, and serve you. Help them to be living examples of the Christian faith, within their family, and in the Church of your dear Son.

At the baptism of all

Bless also your whole Church and this congregation. Strengthen us to obey your command to go forth and make disciples, to baptize them in your name, and to teach the gospel of Christ. Continue to enrich our life together and to add to the number of the faithful those who are being saved until your kingdom is fulfilled. Even so, come, Lord Jesus!

The service of worship shall continue according to the order for the day.

RECEPTION INTO COMMUNICANT MEMBERSHIP

In the Reformed Church in America the Board of Elders alone has authority to receive persons into the communicant membership of the congregation. Such reception may be authorized only on the basis of a candidate's confession of faith in the Lord Jesus Christ, a re-affirmation of such a confession, or the presentation of a satisfactory certificate of transfer from another Christian congregation. Part I of this form may be used by the elders in the exercise of this authority. Part II is for use before the congregation after the elders have granted the request for membership.

PART I: BEFORE THE ELDERS

At the meeting of the elders, the minister or presiding elder shall present each candidate for communicant membership by name. After the presentation the following or another suitable prayer shall be offered.

PRAYER

Let us pray.

O Lord, source of all light and life, you have called us out of the darkness in which we once walked that we might be a people of light. Illumine us now with your wisdom, that what we do at this time may be pleasing in your sight, that your Church may be strengthened and increased, and that your name may be glorified in the midst of your people; through Jesus Christ our Lord. **Amen.**

EXAMINATION OF CANDIDATES

The presiding officer shall begin the examination saying:

N_____ *(use Christian names, omit surnames)*

as baptized Christians, you are already members of Christ's Church, heirs to the covenant of God of which your baptism is the sign and seal. Now you are before us to confess your faith in Christ and to confirm in your own person your willingness to live a Christian life as a communicant member of this congregation. Therefore, I ask you to answer sincerely these questions:

Do you accept the Gospel of God's grace in Jesus Christ revealed in the holy Scriptures of the Old and New Testaments as the only way to eternal life?

I do.

Do you acknowledge that you are a sinner, sinful by nature, but that by the grace of God alone your sins have been forgiven and your old nature put to death, so that you may be brought to newness of life and set apart as a member of the body of Christ?

I do.

Do you promise to pray for yourself and for others, seeking God's guidance as together we seek to grow in knowledge and understanding of the faith?

I do.

Do you promise to show in your own person the joy of new life in Christ by active participation in the life of the Church and by faithful attendance to worship, service, and the offering of prayers and gifts, to the glory of God?

I do.

Do you promise to accept the spiritual guidance of the Church, obeying its doctrines and its teaching, and do you promise to walk in the spirit of Christian love with the congregation, seeking the things that make for unity, purity, and peace?

I do.

The elders may continue the examination, inquiring of individual candidates as to their knowledge and acceptance of the Christian faith and the sincerity of their decisions to become communicant members of the congregation.

Having reached their decision, the elders shall establish the date for public reception of the new communicant members. The meeting shall be concluded with the following or another suitable prayer offered by the presiding officer, with all present joining in the Lord's Prayer.

Let us pray.

Gracious and eternal God, we thank you for the bonds of love we share within your Church, and above all, for Jesus Christ, who has joined us into one living Body. Enable us, by the power of your Spirit, to walk together in unity of love and purpose; to help one another by word and example to live in faithful obedience to your will; and, by the justice and mercy we show toward one another, to give cause always for your name to be praised; through Jesus Christ our Lord,

who has taught us to pray:	*or*	who has taught us when we pray to say:

Our Father in heaven,
   hallowed be your name,
   your kingdom come,
   your will be done,
     on earth as in heaven.
Give us today our daily bread.
Forgive us our sins
   as we forgive those
     who sin against us.
Save us from the time of trial,
   and deliver us from evil.
For the kingdom, the power,
   and the glory are yours,
now and for ever. Amen.

Our Father, who art in heaven,
   hallowed be thy name,
   thy kingdom come,
   thy will be done,
     on earth as it is in heaven.
Give us this day our daily bread.
And forgive us our debts,
   as we forgive our debtors.
And lead us not into temptation,
   but deliver us from evil.
For thine is the kingdom,
   and the power, and the glory,
   for ever. Amen.

PART II: BEFORE THE CONGREGATION

The public confession of faith and reception into the communicant membership of the congregation shall take place on the Lord's Day, during the primary service of worship, after the Word of God has been proclaimed. The elder vice-president of the consistory, or another elder, shall present the candidates using the following form, or with similar words.

PRESENTATION

The elders of the _____ *(name of the church)*

have received into the communicant membership of the congregation _____

_____

_____

_____
(the candidates' full names shall be read in alphabetical order)

who appeared before them, made a sincere confession of their Christian faith, and confirmed their willingness to live within the covenant community of God's people in this church.

I ask them now to come and stand before us so that the whole congregation, hearing them repeat and renew these pledges, may rejoice and welcome them as brothers and sisters in Christ.

The elder and the minister shall stand together, facing the candidates. When all have taken their places, the minister continues:

VOWS

N. _____
_____
(use Christian names, omit surnames)

will you, before God and these your brothers and sisters in Christ, repeat and renew the promises you made when you were accepted into communicant membership in Christ's Church?

I will.

Do you accept the Gospel of God's grace in Jesus Christ revealed in the holy Scriptures of the Old and New Testaments as the only way to eternal life?

I do.

Do you acknowledge that you are a sinner, sinful by nature, but that by the grace of God alone your sins have been forgiven and your old nature put to death, so that you may be brought to newness of life and set apart as a member of the body of Christ?

I do.

Do you promise to pray for yourself and for others, seeking God's guidance as together we seek to grow in knowledge and understanding of the faith?

I do.

Do you promise to show in your own person the joy of new life in Christ by active participation in the life of the Church and by faithful attendance to worship, service, and the offering of prayers and gifts, to the glory of God?

I do.

Do you promise to accept the spiritual guidance of the Church, obeying its doctrines and its teaching, and do you promise to walk in the spirit of Christian love with the congregation, seeking the things that make for unity, purity, and peace?

I do.

When all have risen the minister shall address the congregation:

Do you, the members of this congregation welcome these brothers and sisters into the community of faith as communicant members and pledge to them your love, your prayers, and your encouragement as they live the Christian life with us?

We do.

Let us confess our Christian faith using the Apostles' Creed:

I. THE APOSTLES' CREED

I believe in God, the Father almighty,
  creator of heaven and earth.

I believe in Jesus Christ, his only Son, our Lord.
  He was conceived by the power of the Holy Spirit
    and born of the Virgin Mary.
  He suffered under Pontius Pilate,
    was crucified, died, and was buried.
  He descended to the dead.
  On the third day he rose again.
  He ascended into heaven,
    and is seated at the right hand of the Father.
  He will come again to judge the living and the dead.

I believe in the Holy Spirit,
  the holy catholic Church,
  the communion of saints,
  the forgiveness of sins,
  the resurrection of the body,
  and the life everlasting. Amen.

or

II. THE APOSTLES' CREED

I believe in God, the Father almighty,
   maker of heaven and earth;

And in Jesus Christ, his only Son, our Lord;
   who was conceived by the Holy Ghost,
   born of the Virgin Mary,
   suffered under Pontius Pilate,
   was crucified, dead, and buried.
   He descended into hell.
   The third day he rose again from the dead.
   He ascended into heaven,
   and sitteth on the right hand of God the Father almighty.
   From thence he shall come to judge the quick and the dead.

I believe in the Holy Ghost,
   the holy catholic Church,
   the communion of saints,
   the forgiveness of sins,
   the resurrection of the body,
   and the life everlasting. Amen.

   N.B. A metrical version of the creed may be sung using RIL, hymn 609.

BLESSING

The congregation may be seated. The candidates shall kneel in turn and the minister and elder shall lay a hand on the head of each while the prayer is offered.

Defend, O Lord, this your servant N _____
                                    (use Christian names, omit surname)
_____
with your heavenly grace, that *he   she*   may continue yours forever, and daily increase in your Spirit more and more, until *he   she*   comes to your eternal kingdom; through Jesus Christ our Lord. **Amen.**

PRAYER

After all the candidates have received the laying on of hands, the following or another suitable prayer shall be offered.

Let us pray.

Ever gracious God, sustain and nurture these your children. Make them a blessing to this congregation and to your whole Church. Through the power of the Holy Spirit enable them to serve their Lord faithfully as they live and learn and labor among us and with us.

Grant your grace also to this congregation. Enrich our life together and strengthen our witness to the world in Jesus' name. **Amen.**

   The service of worship shall then continue according to the order appointed. It is most fitting that this include the celebration of the Lord's Supper.

THE ORDINATION AND INSTALLATION
OF ELDERS AND DEACONS

The respective ecclesiastical duties and powers of elders and deacons are laid down in the Book of Church Order (Part 1, Article 1, Sec.'s 7 and 9). These shall be made known to the congregation prior to their election and these officers shall acquaint themselves therewith. Their civil powers vary under the laws of different states.

The BCO (Part I, Article 2, Sec. 10) directs that the names of elders- and deacons- elect shall be published in the church on three successive Sundays preceding their installation in order that lawful objections may be considered.

After an Approach to God, a proclamation of the Word of God, and the reception of the gifts and offerings of the people, the presiding minister shall begin:

PRAYER

Let us pray.

Almighty and everlasting God, who by your Holy Spirit guided the councils of the blessed Apostles and promised, through your Son Jesus Christ, to be with your Church to the end of the world, look upon us in mercy and direct us by your Holy Spirit that what we do at this time may result in the welfare of your kingdom, the building up of your people, and the glory of your Name; through Jesus Christ, our Lord. **Amen.**

EXPOSITION

Brothers and sisters in Christ, you have chosen from among its members persons here present to serve as elders and deacons in this church. Their names have been published several times, and since there is no scriptural reason why they may not be installed into their offices, we shall now proceed in the name of the Lord.

Jesus Christ is the head of his church, which is made up of many members with a variety of gifts. The purpose of these gifts is that the whole church may confess that he is Lord and serve in his name. To enable all of us to do this, he gives particular gifts to some. To the pastor he gives gifts for the ministry of the Word and sacraments; to elders for the ministry of government and discipline; and to deacons for the ministry of compassion and material maintenance. As these ministries are united in Christ, so they are exercised jointly in the church.

Scripture teaches that those chosen to the office of elder are called along with pastors to encourage spiritual growth among the members and help them to walk in the way of Christ. Scripture also teaches that deacons are responsible for the ministry of compassion and material maintenance, representing God's love and mercy in Christ.

By bringing together the offices of pastor, elder, and deacon, the consistory continues the full ministry of Christ in our day. Everything is done decently and in order in the church when faithful persons are chosen for and responsibly carry out these offices.

The presiding minister may recognize by name those persons who have completed their terms of service as elders and deacons, thanking them on behalf of the congregation.

PRESENTATION AND INTERROGATION

The presiding minister shall say:

This congregation has elected _____

_____

(full names)

to fill these offices. I now ask you to stand before us.

When the candidates have done so, the presiding minister continues:

That all may know your willingness to accept these responsibilities, I ask you to answer the following questions:

Do you reaffirm the vows you made when you confessed your faith in Christ and became a communicant member of his Church?

I do.

Do you believe in your heart that you are called by God's Church and therefore by God himself to your respective office?

I do.

Do you believe the books of the Old and New Testaments to be the Word of God and the perfect doctrine of salvation; rejecting all doctrines contrary thereto?

I do.

I ask you who have been elected elders, will you oversee and encourage the spiritual growth of the congregation; providing for the proclamation and hearing of God's Word, the reverent celebration of sacraments, and the loving discipline of the members?

I will, with the help of God.

I ask you who have been elected deacons, will you manifest the love and care of Christ; gathering and distributing the offerings of his people, giving personal attention to the distressed, and exercising good stewardship over the goods and property of the congregation?

I will, with the help of God.

Will you, elders and deacons, be loyal to the witness and work of the Reformed Church in America and do your best to further her mission at home and abroad?

I will.

ORDINATION

If any have not previously been ordained to the office into which they are to be installed, they shall kneel before the presiding minister. All who have been ordained to the office may join the presiding minister in the laying on of hands. During the laying on of hands, the presiding minister shall say:

N_____ *(use Christian names, omit surname)*

by the authority given to his Church by our Lord Jesus Christ, we ordain you *elder deacon,* in the name of the Father, and of the Son, and of the Holy Spirit. **Amen.**

PRAYER

The presiding minister shall offer the following prayer on behalf of all the candidates:

Let us pray.

Most merciful God, who called these persons to these high offices, enlighten them with your Spirit, strengthen them with your hand, and so govern them that their life and labor may be to the glory of your name and the advancement of your kingdom, through Jesus Christ our Lord. **Amen.**

INTERROGATION OF THE CONGREGATION

The presiding minister shall ask the elders- and deacons-elect to face the people and the members of the congregation to rise. When they have done so, the minister shall say:

Do you, the members of this congregation, receive these persons as elders and deacons in Christ's church?

We do.

Will you respect them for the sake of the offices they bear, and promise to walk in the way of the Lord, faithfully heeding Jesus Christ and these servants who represent him?

We will.

The Lord bless you and multiply his grace to enable you to fulfill your promises.

Amen.

DECLARATION

The presiding minister shall ask the elders and deacons to turn about and address them:

In the name of the Lord Jesus Christ, the Head of the Church, I declare that you are now ordained and duly installed in your respective offices, and commend you to the grace of God which will enable you to discharge all your duties. The Lord bless you and keep you: The Lord make his face to shine upon you and be gracious to you: The Lord lift up the light of his countenance upon you and give you peace. The grace of the Lord Jesus Christ be with you always.

Amen.

75669

EXHORTATION

Elders and deacons, I call upon you to be faithful in performing your duties, to magnify the Lord and show zeal for his church, for which he shed his own blood.

Brothers and sisters, receive these persons as you would receive Christ. Support them in love, that their work may be productive, and together we may serve the Lord and experience his blessings. Let us pray for one another that each may obtain whatever grace we need to fulfill our duties.

The following or a similar prayer may be offered at this point or incorporated in the General Prayers:

Let us pray.

Almighty and merciful God, of whose help and guidance we always stand in need, bestow upon your servants such gifts as are necessary for them in their respective ministries. Give grace to them that they may serve you faithfully in this life and finally enter into the joy of the life to come.

Grant your grace also to your people whom they serve, so that all of us may fulfill our ministry, magnifying your name and increasing the kingdom of your Son, Jesus Christ; in whose name we pray. **Amen.**

Then may follow the GENERAL PRAYERS and the LORD'S PRAYER, unless it has been used already in the service. A HYMN of Thanksgiving may be sung. The service shall conclude with the BENEDICTION.

PREPARATORY EXHORTATION BEFORE THE CELEBRATION OF THE LORD'S SUPPER

A preparatory service may be held before each celebration of the Lord's Supper, in connection with the Communion service itself, or on the previous Sunday. It may be observed in the worship service just prior to the Prayer of Confession, replacing the normal invitation to pray. The following exhortation may be used to meet the requirement.

EXHORTATION TO SELF-EXAMINATION

Beloved in the Lord Jesus Christ, we propose to celebrate together, with the gracious help of God, the Sacrament of the Lord's Supper *this next* Lord's Day. That we may celebrate this Sacrament to our comfort, it is necessary that we rightly examine ourselves. Let us all, therefore, consider our sins, asking ourselves whether we believe this faithful promise of God: that all our sins are forgiven us only for the sake of the passion and death of Jesus Christ, and that the perfect righteousness of Christ is freely given to us as our own, even as perfectly as if we had fulfilled all righteousness. Let us also ask ourselves whether we make it our aim to show true thankfulness to God in our whole life, to walk uprightly before God, and to live in love and peace with our neighbor.

All those who are of this mind God will certainly receive in mercy and count them worthy partakers of the Supper of our Lord. On the contrary, according to the command of Christ and the Apostle Paul, we admonish all those who are continuing in unrepented sin to keep themselves from the Lord's Table.

This admonition is not intended, dearly beloved, to distress the contrite hearts of God's people, as if none might come to our Lord's Table but those who are without sin. For we do not come to this Supper to testify that we are righteous in ourselves, but rather that we are conscious of our sinfulness and trust in Jesus Christ alone for our salvation.

Therefore, despite any feeling that we do not have perfect faith, and that we do not serve God with such zeal as we ought, but have daily to strive with the weakness of our faith and the selfishness of our desires; yet since we are, by the grace of the Holy Spirit, sorry for these weaknesses and earnest in our desire to fight against our unbelief and to live according to all the commandments of God, therefore we rest assured that no sin or infirmity which still remains against our will in us can hinder us from being received by God in mercy and from being made worthy partakers of our Lord.

That we may now so examine ourselves before almighty God, let us confess our sins. Let us pray.

PRAYER OF CONFESSION

All shall join in making the personal and corporate acknowledgement of sin and of their continuing need for God's redemptive grace. A brief period for silent prayers may follow the corporate confession.

PART II
Occasional
Services

ORDER OF WORSHIP
FOR CHRISTIAN MARRIAGE

THE APPROACH TO GOD

The service of worship may begin with instrumental and/or choral music in praise of God. When the wedding party has assembled they may approach the front of the church during a

PROCESSIONAL HYMN

All present shall stand to sing, and remain standing through the Salutation.

VOTUM

Our help is in the name of the LORD who made heaven and earth. **Amen.**

SENTENCES

One of the following or another appropriate scriptural sentence shall be read.

I will sing of the LORD'S great love forever;

with my mouth I will make your faithfulness known to all generations.

I will declare that your love stands firm forever,

that you established your faithfulness in heaven itself.   *Psalm 89:1-2*

or

O servants of the LORD, you that stand in the house of the LORD, in the courts of the house of our God! Praise the LORD, for the LORD is good; sing to his name, for he is gracious!   *Psalm 135:1b-3*

SALUTATION

Grace and peace be yours in fullest measure, through the knowledge of God and Jesus our Lord. **Amen.**   *II Peter 1:2*

DECLARATION OF PURPOSE

After the people have been seated, the minister shall say:

We are gathered here to praise God for the covenant of grace and reconciliation made with us through Jesus Christ, to hear it proclaimed anew, and to respond to it as we witness the covenant of marriage N. N. _____ and N. N. _____ make with each other in Christ's name.

Christian marriage is a joyful covenanting between a man and a woman in which they proclaim, before God and human witnesses, their commitment to live together in spiritual, physical, and material unity. In this covenant they acknowledge that the great love God has shown for each of them enables them to love each other. They affirm that God's gracious presence and abiding power are needed for them to keep their vows, to continue to live in love, and to be faithful servants of Christ in this world. For human commitment is fragile and human love imperfect, but the promise of God is eternal and the love of God can bring our love to perfection.

THE WORD OF GOD

PRAYER

Let us pray.

Most gracious God, be with us in this time of joy and celebration. Reveal **the** good news of your love for us in the proclamation of your Word. Enable **us** to respond to you with faithfulness and obedience, so that in all we do and say your name may be praised. Through Jesus Christ our Lord we pray. **Amen.**

LESSONS

One or more lessons from Scripture shall be read. If there is only one lesson, it shall be from the New Testament.

Old Testament: Genesis 1:26-28, 31a; Psalm 22:25-31; Psalm 37:3-6; Isaiah 61:1-3, 10-11

Epistle: I Corinthians 12:31-13:8a; Ephesians 3:14-21; Colossians 3:12-17; I John 4:7-16

Gospel: Matthew 5:13-16; Luke 6:36-38; John 2:1-11; John 15:9-14

SERMON

The minister may preach a brief sermon relating the Word of God to the response of Christian Marriage.

PRAYER FOR BLESSING

Almighty God, through your grace write these words in our hearts, that they may bring forth in us the fruits of the Spirit, to the honor and praise of your name, through Jesus Christ our Lord. **Amen.**

THE RESPONSE TO GOD

DECLARATION OF CONSENT

The persons to be married shall stand with their attendants before the minister, who shall ask the man:

N. _____ will you receive N. _____ as your wife and bind yourself to her in the covenant of marriage? Will you promise to love and honor her in true devotion; to rejoice with her in times of felicity and grieve with her in times of sorrow; and be faithful to her as long as you both shall live?

I will, with the help of God.

The minister shall ask the woman:

N. _____ will you receive N. _____ as your husband and bind yourself to him in the covenant of marriage? Will you promise to love and honor him in true devotion; to rejoice with him in times of felicity and grieve with him in times of sorrow; and be faithful to him as long as you both shall live?

I will, with the help of God.

The minister shall ask the family members of the persons to be married to stand. When they have done so, the minister shall ask:

Will you receive N. _____ and N. _____ into your family and uphold them with your love as they establish themselves as a family within your own?

We will.

The minister shall ask all present to stand. When they have done so, the minister shall ask:

Will you who witness this covenant between N. _____ and N. _____ respect their marriage and sustain them with your friendship and care?

We will.

VOWS

The minister shall say to the man and the woman:

N. _____ and N. _____, before God and these witnesses, make your covenant of marriage with each other.

Vows may be exchanged according to Form I or Form II below.

Form I

The man shall face the woman, take her hand in his, and say:

I, N. _____ take you, N. _____, to be my wife,
to have and to hold from this day forward,
for better, for worse,
for richer, for poorer,
in sickness and in health,
to love and to cherish
as long as we both shall live.
To this I pledge myself
truly with all my heart.

The minister shall receive the ring from its bearer and give it to the man, who shall place it on the hand of the woman and say:

This ring I give in token of the covenant made this day between us; in the name of the Father and of the Son and of the Holy Spirit.

The woman, still facing the man and taking his hand in hers, shall say:

I, N. _____ take you, N. _____, to be my husband,
to have and to hold from this day forward,
for better, for worse,
for richer, for poorer,
in sickness and in health,
to love and to cherish
as long as we both shall live.
To this I pledge myself
truly with all my heart.

The minister shall receive the ring from its bearer and give it to the woman, who shall place it on the hand of the man and say:

This ring I give in token of the covenant made this day between us; in the name of the Father and of the Son and of the Holy Spirit.

or

Form II

The man and the woman shall face each other and take hands. They shall say to each other, in turn:

N. _____,
I give myself to you in marriage
and vow to be your   husband   wife
all the days of our lives.

I give you my hands
and take your hands in mine
as a symbol and pledge
of our uniting in one flesh.

I give you my love,
the outpouring of my heart,
as a symbol and pledge
of our uniting in one spirit.

I give you this ring
from out of my worldly goods
as a symbol and pledge
of our uniting as one family.

After each has said the vows, he/she shall take the ring from the minister and place it on the other's hand.

BLESSING

Prayer may be offered according to Form I or Form II. The minister may ask the married persons to kneel, or to remain standing and face the minister.

Form I

Let us ask for the blessing of the Lord.

Eternal God,
in whom we live and move and have our being;
bless N. _____ and N. _____
that they may live together in marriage
according to the vows they have made before you.

Bless them with your love,
that their love for each other
may grow ever deeper,
and their love for you may shine forth
before the world.

Bless them with your mercy,
that they may be patient and caring,
willing to share each other's joys and sorrows,
to forgive and to be forgiven,
in their life together and in the world.

Bless them with your peace,
that they may be calm and sure,
trusting in you with confident hearts
and living in harmony and concord
within their family and among all people.

Bless them with your presence,
that within their hearts and their home
Christ may reign as head,
and that they may acknowledge his Lordship
with praise and thanksgiving
now, and through all their life together,
to the glory of your holy name! **Amen.**

or

34 ORDER OF WORSHIP FOR CHRISTIAN MARRIAGE

Form II

Let us pray.

O God, Creator of life, Author of Salvation and Giver of all good gifts; look with favor upon N. _____ and N. _____ who have covenanted marriage in your name. Bless their union, and sustain them in their devotion to each other and to you.

Grant them the desire to order their lives according to your will, that in their relationship with each other, and those around them, they may show forth the joy and peace of Christ.

Sustain them in the seasons and conditions of their lives by the power of your Holy Spirit, that in joy and sorrow, leisure and labor, plenty and want, they may give thanks for your steadfast love and declare your faithfulness before the world.

Increase in them the will to grow in faith and service to Christ. Let their life together bear witness to the healing and reconciling love of Christ for this troubled, broken world.

Give them a deep appreciation of the unity of all persons within your creation, that their love for each other may be reflected also in their desire for justice, dignity and meaning for all your children.

Keep ever vivid in their hearts a vision of your kingdom, and enable them to live in the hope of its fulfillment. By the power of your Spirit, O God, accomplish these petitions as they accord with your will, for we pray through Jesus Christ our Lord. **Amen.**

DECLARATION

N. _____ and N. _____ have made their covenant of marriage together before God and all here present, by solemn vows, by the joining of hands, and the giving and receiving of rings. Therefore, I declare that they are husband and wife; in the name of the Father and of the Son and of the Holy Spirit.

    and (to the couple)
Be united; live in peace, and the God of peace and love will be with you.
                                      II Corinthians 12:11

    or (to all present)

They are no longer two, therefore, but one body. So then, what God has united, no one may divide. **Amen.**   *Matthew 19:6*

PEACE

The husband and wife greet each other with the kiss of peace.

BENEDICTION

The grace of the Lord Jesus Christ, the love of God, and the fellowship of the Holy Spirit be with you all. **Amen.**   *II Corinthians 12:13*

RECESSIONAL HYMN

A hymn of thanksgiving may be sung, or instrumental music played, during which the married persons and their attendants may recess.

ORDERS FOR
CHRISTIAN HEALING

IN THE CONTEXT OF THE ORDER OF WORSHIP

THE APPROACH TO GOD

> VOTUM
> SENTENCES
> SALUTATION
> HYMN
> PRAYER OF CONFESSION

The minister may introduce the prayer with one of the following or another suitable call to confession.

Blessed is he whose transgressions are forgiven, whose sins are covered. When I kept silent, my bones wasted away through my groaning all day long. Then I acknowledged my sin to you and did not cover up my iniquity. I said, "I will confess my transgressions to the LORD"—and you forgave the guilt of my sin. *Psalm 32:1, 3, 5*

> *or*

If we say we have no sin, we deceive ourselves, and the truth is not in us. If we confess our sins, he is faithful and just, and will forgive our sins and cleanse us from all unrighteousness. *1 John 1:8-9*

> *and*

Let us confess our sin to almighty God. Let us pray.

Have mercy upon us, O God, according to your loving-kindness: according unto the multitude of your tender mercies, blot out our transgressions. Wash us thoroughly from our iniquity and cleanse us from our sin, for we acknowledge our transgressions, and our sin is ever before us. Create in us a clean heart, O God, and renew a right spirit within us. Cast us not away from your presence, and take not your Holy Spirit from us. Restore unto us the joy of your salvation, and uphold us with your free spirit; through Jesus Christ our Lord. Amen. *Adapted from Psalm 51*

> *or*

Merciful God, in compassion for your sinful children you sent your Son Jesus Christ to be the savior of the world. Grant us grace to confess the sin which made it needful for him to be broken that we might be made whole, to be troubled in spirit that we might be given peace, to be put to death on the cross that we might be restored to life.

> *A brief period of silent confession may be allowed, after which the prayer shall continue.*

Give us a true longing to be free from sin, and a true willingness to follow him who stooped to our need and who raises us up from the misery of sin to the wholeness of forgiven life, even Jesus Christ our Lord in whose name we pray. Amen.

ASSURANCE OF PARDON

Bless the LORD, O my soul; and all that is within me, bless his holy name! Bless the LORD, O my soul, and forget not all his benefits, who forgives all your iniquity, who heals all your diseases, who redeems your life from the Pit.   *Psalm 103:1-4a*

or Psalm 30:1-3, Psalm 41:1-3, Ephesians 2:1-7 (8-10)

LAW OF GOD AND/OR SUMMARY OF THE LAW
PSALTER AND GLORIA

THE WORD OF GOD

PRAYER FOR ILLUMINATION
HYMN
LESSONS
SERMON
PRAYER FOR BLESSING ON THE WORD
CONFESSION OF FAITH
OFFERING
DOXOLOGY
THE SACRAMENT OF THE LORD'S SUPPER

When the Sacrament is celebrated the following may be used in place of the Prayers of Intercession. When it is not celebrated, this Litany and Prayer of Thanksgiving may be used in place of the General Prayers.

THE RESPONSE TO GOD

LITANY OF INTERCESSION FOR HEALING

O God the Father, whose will for us and for all your people is health and salvation;

Have mercy on us.

O God the Son, who came that we might have life and have it in abundance;

Have mercy on us.

O God the Holy Spirit, whose indwelling makes our bodies the temples of your presence;

Have mercy on us.

O Triune God, we pray you to hear us, and that you will grant your grace to all who stand in need of healing both of body and spirit, and lead them to look with confidence to you;

We beseech you to hear us, O Lord.

That you will grant patience and perseverance to all who are disabled by injury or illness, and increase their courage;

We beseech you to hear us, O Lord.

That you will grant peace to all who are troubled by confusion or pain, and set their minds at rest;

We beseech you to hear us, O Lord.

That you will grant relief from suffering to all sick children, and give them a sure sense of your tender love and care;

We beseech you to hear us, O Lord.

That you will grant rest to all whose increasing years bring weariness, distress or loneliness, and give them the abiding comfort of your presence;

We beseech you to hear us, O Lord.

That you will grant confidence to all about to undergo surgery or difficult procedures, and keep them free from fear;

We beseech you to hear us, O Lord.

That you will grant purpose to the Church as it seeks to carry on Christ's ministry of healing to suffering humanity, and keep it always true to the Gospel of Christ;

We beseech you to hear us, O Lord.

That you will grant skill and compassion to doctors, nurses, technicians, aides, and all who are called to practice medical arts, and make strong their dedication to help others;

We beseech you to hear us, O Lord.

That you will grant to all people the refreshment of quiet sleep and joy of resting in your everlasting arms, that we may rejoice in your care while we are on earth, and in the world to come have eternal life;

We beseech you to hear us, O Lord.

> *The Litany may continue with petitions for specific needs of the people. It may conclude with the following ascription:*

O God, who in Jesus Christ called us out of the darkness into your marvelous light; enable us always to declare your wonderful deeds, thank you for your steadfast love, and praise you with heart, soul, mind, and strength, now and forever. **Amen.**

LAYING ON OF HANDS AND ANOINTING WITH OIL

Luke 9:1-2 and/or James 5:13-16 shall be read: After which the minister shall invite worshipers to receive the laying on of hands and anointing with oil using these or similar words:

In the name of the Lord Jesus who sent forth his disciples to preach the kingdom of God and to heal, we invite you who wish to receive the laying on of hands and the anointing with oil to come forward or summon us to come to your side.

We invite all here present to participate in this act of faith through the offering of silent prayers for those who seek Christian healing.

Since healing is a ministry of the church it is appropriate that the minister be joined by one or two elders, or such persons as the board of elders may designate, for the laying on of hands. The minister or an elder may also anoint the worshiper with oil following the blessing.

May the hands of the Great Physician, Jesus Christ, rest upon you now in divine blessing and healing. May the cleansing stream of his pure life fill your whole being, body, mind and spirit, to strengthen and heal you. **Amen.**

or

Eternal God, for Jesus' sake, send your Holy Spirit upon your servant N. _____: drive away all sickness of body and spirit; make whole that which is broken. Grant deliverance from the power of evil, and true faith in Jesus Christ our Lord, who suffered on our behalf but also rose from death so that we, too, could live. In his name we pray. **Amen.**

A brief silence may be kept after the last worshiper has been anointed.

PRAYER OF THANKSGIVING:

After all have returned to their places the minister may offer the following or another appropriate thanksgiving prayer.

Most gracious God, source of all healing; we give thanks to you for all your gifts but most of all for the gift of your Son, through whom you gave and still give health and salvation to all who believe. As we wait in expectation for the coming of that day when suffering and pain shall be no more, help us by your Holy Spirit to be assured of your power in our lives and to trust in your eternal love, through Jesus Christ our Lord. **Amen.**

HYMN
BENEDICTION

* * * * *

ON OTHER OCCASIONS

VOTUM, SENTENCES, SALUTATION
HYMN OF PRAISE
WORD OF EXPLANATION:

It is appropriate that the worship leader explain the nature of a service of Christian healing, emphasizing God's presence and power to strengthen and support and bring increasing wholeness to his people.

PSALMS/HYMNS
LESSON(S)
BRIEF SERMON
PRAYERS OF CONFESSION AND SELF-EXAMINATION
INTERCESSIONS
LAYING ON OF HANDS AND ANOINTING WITH OIL
HYMN (OR PRAYER) OF THANKSGIVING
BENEDICTION

* * * * *

IN HOME OR HOSPITAL VISITATION

Ministers, elders, deacons, or other visitors should use this service with sensitivity to the specific needs of the person(s) being visited and after ascertaining their willingness to participate in this act of faith. It would be most appropriate to use this service after a preliminary conversation and expression of pastoral concern.

SALUTATION

Grace and peace to you from God our Father and Christ Jesus our Lord. We are here in the name of the Lord Jesus whose ministry to God's people was one of healing power and saving grace. He promised those who believe in him that he would be with them always, and his promise is true. He is present among us still to heal and to make whole.

CONFESSION OF SIN

Now in the presence of the Lord, let us confess our sins. Let us pray.

Silence may be kept, after which one of the visitors may offer the following, or another prayer.

O God, who hears our prayers before we speak them, who knows our needs before we raise them up; you have heard the confession of our hearts. Now grant us your mercy and forgiveness through Jesus Christ our Lord, who came into the world to rescue us from sin and bring us to life in him. **Amen.**

ASSURANCE OF PARDON

The following, or another scriptural assurance may be read.

With everlasting love I will have compassion on you, says the Lord your Redeemer. I, I am he who blots out your transgressions for my own sake, and I will not remember your sins. Return to me, for I have redeemed you.

Isaiah 54:8, 43:35, 44:22

PRAYERS OF INTERCESSION

Prayers may be offered for the person being visited asking for God's healing love and tender care to be granted in Christ's name. The prayers may be concluded with the following petition:

O God, who in Jesus Christ called us out of the darkness into your marvelous light; enable us always to declare your wonderful deeds, thank you for your steadfast love, and praise you with heart, soul, mind, and strength, now and forever. **Amen.**

LESSONS

One or more brief passages of Scripture may be read. Those cited in the Order for the Visitation of the Sick, Liturgy 1968 (pp. 170-1) may be especially appropriate. One or both of the following lessons shall be read:

And [Jesus] called the twelve together and gave them power and authority over all demons and to cure diseases, and he sent them out to preach the kingdom of God and to heal.   *Luke 9:1-2*

    and/or

Is any one of you in trouble? He should pray. Is any one happy? Let him sing songs of praise. Is any one of you sick? He should call the elders of the church to pray over him and anoint him with oil in the name of the Lord, and the prayer offered in faith will make the sick person well; the Lord will raise him up. If he has sinned, he will be forgiven.   *James 5:13-15 NIV*

LAYING ON OF HANDS AND ANOINTING WITH OIL

The pastoral visitors shall lay hands on the head of the sick person. One of them may say one of the following after which the sick person may be anointed with oil.

May the hands of the Great Physician, Jesus Christ, rest upon you now in divine blessing and healing. May the cleansing stream of his pure life fill your whole being, body, mind and spirit, to strengthen and heal you. **Amen.**

    or

Eternal God, for Jesus' sake, send your Holy Spirit upon your servant N. _____; drive away all sickness of body and spirit; make whole that which is broken. Grant deliverance from the power of evil, and true faith in Jesus Christ our Lord, who suffered on our behalf, but also rose from death so that we, too, could live. In his name we pray. **Amen.**

A brief silence may be kept, after the sick person has been anointed.

PRAYER OF THANKSGIVING

Let us give thanks to the Lord. Let us pray.

Most gracious God, source of all healing; we give thanks to you for all your gifts but most of all for the gift of your Son, through whom you gave and still give health and salvation to all who believe. As we wait in expectation for the coming of that day when suffering and pain shall be no more, help us by your Holy Spirit to be assured of your power in our lives and to trust in your eternal love, through Jesus Christ our Lord. **Amen.**

BENEDICTION

ORDER OF WORSHIP
FOR CHRISTIAN BURIAL

The Order of Worship for Christian Burial should be conducted in the church, preferably at a time when the congregation can be present. The casket should be closed before the service and thereafter remain closed. It may be appropriate that it be covered with a pall or other suitable covering. If there are to be flowers at the church, they should be limited in number.

THE APPROACH TO GOD

VOTUM

Our help is in the name of the LORD, who made heaven and earth. **Amen.**

or

In the name of the Father and of the Son and of the Holy Spirit. **Amen.**

SENTENCES

Come to me, all who labor and are heavy laden, and I will give you rest. Take my yoke upon you, and learn from me; for I am gentle and lowly in heart, and you will find rest for your souls.   *Matthew 11:28-29*

or

I am the resurrection and the life, says the Lord; whoever believes in me, though he die, yet shall he live, and whoever lives and believes in me shall never die.   *John 11:25-26*

or

Another appropriate passage, such as Job 1:21; Romans 14:7-9; John 14:25-27.

SALUTATION

Grace to you and peace from God our Father and the Lord Jesus Christ. **Amen.**

or

Grace to you and peace from him who is and was and who is to come, and from Jesus Christ the faithful witness, the first-born of the dead, and the ruler of the kings on earth.

To him who loves us and has freed us from our sins by his blood and made us a kingdom, priests to his God and Father, to him be glory and dominion for ever and ever. Amen.   *Revelation 1:4b-6*

A Hymn may be sung or the service may proceed to the Confession or the Prayer of Illumination.

PRAYER OF CONFESSION

Eternal God, before whose face the generations rise and pass away, you formed us in your image and willed us to live before you in peace and love. We confess we are not the people you created or called us to be—we have not loved you with our whole heart or our neighbors as ourselves. Forgive

our sin, O God, and create in us a new and willing spirit, so that in our living, we may serve you, and in our dying, enter the joy of your presence, through Jesus Christ our Lord.

and

Lord, have mercy upon us.
Christ, have mercy upon us.
Lord, have mercy upon us.

ASSURANCE OF PARDON

With everlasting love I will have compassion on you, says the Lord your Redeemer. I, I am he who blots out your transgressions for my own sake, and I will not remember your sins. Return to me, for I have redeemed you. In the name of the Father, and of the Son, and of the Holy Spirit. **Amen.**

or

Who is in a position to condemn? Only Christ, and Christ died for us, Christ rose for us, Christ reigns in power for us, Christ prays for us. Hear and believe the good news of the Gospel: God is love, and in his love we are forgiven. **Amen.**

or

For God so loved the world that he gave his only Son, that whoever believes in him should not perish, but have eternal life. For God sent the Son into the world, not to condemn the world, but that the world might be saved through him.   *John 3:16, 17*

May the God and Father of our Lord Jesus Christ pardon all our sins. **Amen.**

THE WORD OF GOD

PRAYER OF ILLUMINATION

Let us pray.

Eternal God, our refuge and our strength, console and support those who are sorrowful through the comfort of your Word, so we might be confident in this and every time of need, trusting in your love; through Jesus Christ our Lord. **Amen.**

or

Almighty God, whose love never fails, and who can turn the shadow of death into the light of life, illumine us through your Word; so that hearing your promises, we may be lifted out of darkness and distress into the light and peace of your presence, through Jesus Christ our Lord. **Amen.**

LESSONS

There will ordinarily be two or three lessons, one from the Old Testament, one from the portion of the New Testament other than the Gospels, and one from the Gospels.

Old Testament—Psalm 23; 27; 42:11-43:5; 84:1-4, 8-12; 121

The reading may be followed by the Gloria Patri:

Glory be to the Father, and to the Son, and to the Holy Spirit: as it was in the beginning, is now, and ever shall be, world without end. Amen.

Epistle: Romans 8:28 (29-30), 31-35, 37-39; I Corinthians 15:49-57; II Corinthians 4:5-18; Philippians 2:1-11; Hebrews 12:18-24; Revelation 7:9-17

Gospel: Matthew 6:25-33; Mark 5:22-42; Luke 24:1-8, 36-43; John 1:1-5, 9-14; John 6:25-40, 47-51; John 14:1-6, 18, 19, 25-27

SERMON

A brief sermon may be preached. The focus of the sermon is the hope set before us in the Gospel: that in life, in death, in life beyond death, God is with us. It may also be appropriate to acknowledge this hope as it was manifested in the life of the one who has died in the faith.

ASCRIPTION OF PRAISE

Now to the one who is able to keep you from falling, to present you faultless before the presence of his glory with exceeding joy,

To the only wise God our Savior, be glory and majesty, dominion and power, both now and for ever. **Amen.**

A Hymn may be sung.

THE RESPONSE TO GOD

CONFESSION OF FAITH

Let us confess our Christian faith . . .

I. THE APOSTLES' CREED

I believe in God, the Father almighty,
  creator of heaven and earth.

I believe in Jesus Christ, his only Son, our Lord.
  He was conceived by the power of the Holy Spirit
    and born of the Virgin Mary.
  He suffered under Pontius Pilate,
    was crucified, died, and was buried.
  He descended to the dead.
  On the third day he rose again.
  He ascended into heaven,
    and is seated at the right hand of the Father.
  He will come again to judge the living and the dead.

I believe in the Holy Spirit,
  the holy catholic Church,
  the communion of saints,
  the forgiveness of sins,
  the resurrection of the body,
  and the life everlasting. Amen.

or

II. THE APOSTLES' CREED

I believe in God, the Father almighty,
   maker of heaven and earth;

And in Jesus Christ, his only Son, our Lord;
   who was conceived by the Holy Ghost,
   born of the Virgin Mary,
   suffered under Pontius Pilate,
   was crucified, dead, and buried.
   He descended into hell.
   The third day he rose again from the dead.
   He ascended into heaven,
   and sitteth on the right hand of God the Father almighty.
   From thence he shall come to judge the quick and the dead.

I believe in the Holy Ghost,
   the holy catholic Church,
   the communion of saints,
   the forgiveness of sins,
   the resurrection of the body,
   and the life everlasting. Amen.

N.B. A metrical version of the creed may be sung using RIL, hymn 609.

or

What then shall we say to this?
If God is for us, who is against us?
Who shall separate us from the love of Christ?
Shall tribulation, or distress, or persecution,
or famine, or nakedness,
or peril or sword?

No, in all these things we are more than conquerors
through him who loved us.
For I am sure that neither death, nor life,
nor angels, nor principalities,
nor things present, nor things to come,
nor powers, nor height, nor depth,
nor anything else in all creation,
will be able to separate us from the love
of God in Christ Jesus our Lord.   *Romans 8:31, 35, 37-39*

PRAYERS OF THANKSGIVING AND INTERCESSION

Let us pray.

O God, from the dawn of the first day you have cared for your people. By your hand we were created; in your hand we live; and to your hand we return again. You have revealed yourself in many and various ways, until, in the fullness of time, your word was made flesh and dwelt among us in the person of Jesus Christ our Lord. In his life, death, and resurrection we find our calling in this world and our hope for the world to come.

Therefore with your whole Church on earth and with all the company of heaven we worship and adore your glorious name:

Holy, holy, holy Lord, God of hosts. Heaven and earth are full of your glory. Hosanna in the highest! Blessed is he that comes in the name of the Lord. Hosanna in the highest!

O God, you understand our grief, for you have felt our pain. Jesus wept with Mary and Martha at the death of Lazarus, and the heavens were darkened when your own Son died upon the cross. Comfort us with the knowledge that Jesus raised his friend and will raise all who hear his voice, for he destroyed the darkness of death when you raised him to the light of Easter morn.

We give you thanks in this day for your servants, who, having lived this life in faith, now live eternally with you. Especially we thank you for N. _____, for the gift of *his* *her* life, for the grace you have given *him* *her*, for all in *him* *her* that was good and kind and faithful. *(Here mention may be made of attributes or service.)* We thank you that for *him* *her* death is past, and pain is ended, and *he* *she* has entered the joy you have prepared in the company of all the saints.

Give us faith to look beyond touch and sight, and in seeing that we are surrounded by so great a cloud of witnesses, enable us to run with perseverance the race that is set before us, looking to Jesus, the author and finisher of our faith. Bring us at last to your eternal peace, through Jesus Christ our Lord, in whose name we are bold to pray:

LORD'S PRAYER

Our Father in heaven,
  hallowed be your name,
  your kingdom come,
  your will be done,
    on earth as in heaven.
Give us today our daily bread.
Forgive us our sins
  as we forgive those
  who sin against us.
Save us from the time of trial,
  and deliver us from evil.
For the kingdom, the power,
  and the glory are yours,
now and for ever. Amen.

Our Father, who art in heaven,
  hallowed be thy name,
  thy kingdom come,
  thy will be done,
    on earth as it is in heaven.
Give us this day our daily bread.
And forgive us our debts,
  as we forgive our debtors.
And lead us not into temptation,
  but deliver us from evil.
For thine is the kingdom,
  and the power, and the glory,
  for ever. Amen.

COMMENDATION

Into your hands, O merciful Savior, we commend your servant N. _____. Acknowledge, we pray, a sheep of your fold, a lamb of your own flock, a sinner of your own redeeming. Receive *him* *her* into the arms of your mercy, into the blessed rest of everlasting peace, and into the glorious company of the saints in light.

Let us go forth in the name of Christ. **Amen.**

A Hymn may be sung.

If the body is to be committed for burial, the service shall continue at the grave.

THE COMMITTAL

And I heard a voice from heaven saying, "Write this: Blessed are the dead who die in the Lord." "Blessed indeed," says the Spirit, "that they may rest from their labors, for their deeds follow them!" *Rev. 14:13*

or

I lift up my eyes to the hills. From whence does my help come? My help comes from the LORD, who made heaven and earth. He will not let your foot be moved, he who keeps you will not slumber. Behold, he who keeps Israel will neither slumber nor sleep. The LORD is your keeper; the LORD is your shade on your right hand. The sun shall not smite you by day, nor the moon by night. The LORD will keep you from all evil; he will keep your life. The LORD will keep your going out and your coming in from this time forth and for evermore. *Psalm 121*

or

Then I saw a new heaven and a new earth; for the first heaven and the first earth had passed away, and the sea was no more. And I saw the holy city, new Jerusalem, coming down out of heaven from God, prepared as a bride adorned for her husband; and I heard a loud voice from the throne saying, "Behold, the dwelling of God is with men. God will dwell with them, and they shall be his people, and God himself will be with them; he will wipe away every tear from their eyes, and death shall be no more, neither shall there be mourning nor crying nor pain any more, for the former things have passed away." *Rev. 21:1-4*

COMMITTAL

As the body is committed to the grave, earth may be cast upon the coffin by the minister and/or the family and friends of the deceased.

We have entrusted our *brother   sister,* N. _____, into the hands of God, and we now commit *his   her* body to the *ground deep   elements   this resting place,*   earth to earth, ashes to ashes, dust to dust, in sure and certain hope of the resurrection to eternal life through our Lord Jesus Christ. The Lord bless *him   her* and keep *him   her,* the Lord make his face to shine upon *him   her* and be gracious unto *him   her,* the Lord lift up his countenance upon *him   her* and grant *him   her* peace. **Amen.**

PRAYER

Let us pray.

O God, in the beginning you formed us from the dust of the earth and breathed into us the breath of life. So also, in these last days, you have promised to raise us from the dust, so we might assume a new body at the coming of your Son. For as in Adam all die, so in Christ shall all be made alive. We thank you for this hope kindled within our hearts, that N. _____, who has died, will in the twinkling of an eye be raised to life imperishable.

Look down with tender pity and compassion upon us in this day, and grant unto each of us the comfort of your spirit. Renew within us the gifts of faith, hope, and love, through Jesus Christ our Lord, who lives and reigns with you and the Holy Spirit, world without end. **Amen.**

BENEDICTION

Now the God of peace who brought again from the dead our Lord Jesus, the great Shepherd of the sheep, by the blood of the eternal covenant, equip you with everything good that you may do his will, working in you that which is pleasing in his sight, through Jesus Christ; to whom be glory forever and ever. And the blessing of God Almighty, Father, Son, and Holy Spirit be and abide with you always. **Amen.**

PART III
Classical
Services

THE ORDINATION AND INSTALLATION OF A MINISTER OF THE WORD

The Book of Church Order (Part II, Article 10, Section 5) directs the classis to appoint a time for the ordination service of candidates for the ministry and to conduct the service, in regular or special session, with proper solemnity. A sermon suitable to the occasion shall be preached.

If the candidate also is to be installed as the pastor and teacher of a congregation, the Book of Church Order further directs (Part I, Article 2, Section 2) that after a call has been approved by the classis and accepted by the person called, "the latter's name shall be published in the church on three successive Sundays, so that opportunity may be afforded for the raising of lawful objections." There being none, the classis shall proceed with the installation.

After the sermon has been preached, the presiding officer of the classis shall begin:

PRAYER

Let us pray.

O God, the great shepherd of the Church, who through the light of your Holy Spirit has always guided your people: grant that we, by the same Spirit, may live for you, and together with all whom you call to serve within the body of Christ, may be faithful and obedient to your Word, through Jesus Christ our Lord. **Amen.**

EXPOSITION

Beloved in the Lord, Holy Scripture teaches us that God our heavenly Father gathers to himself from among the lost children of this world a Church to life eternal, and that in this work of grace he is pleased to use our ministry. The Lord Jesus himself provides us with the grace we need to serve him, as affirmed by the Apostle Paul: "And his gifts were that some should be apostles, some prophets, some evangelists, some pastors and teachers, to equip the saints for the work of ministry, for building up the body of Christ."

Ephesians 4:11-12

INTERROGATION

The presiding officer shall ask the candidate to stand before the congregation.

N. N., _____ *(using full name)*
the Classis of _____ has examined you and has found you to be qualified as a person of sound learning and of Christian character, well suited to exercise the ministry of the Word within the Church of Christ. That it may be clear to all here present that you are willing to accept this office and fulfill the ministry to which you have been called, you are to answer sincerely to these questions:

Do you confess with us and the Church throughout all ages your faith in one God, Father, Son, and Holy Spirit?

I do.

The presiding officer shall invite the congregation to stand:

Let us all arise and stand with N. _____ *(use Christian names,*
omit surname) confessing our Christian faith in the words of the Apostles' Creed.

I. THE APOSTLES' CREED

I believe in God, the Father almighty,
    creator of heaven and earth.

I believe in Jesus Christ, his only Son, our Lord.
    He was conceived by the power of the Holy Spirit
        and born of the Virgin Mary.
    He suffered under Pontius Pilate,
        was crucified, died, and was buried.
    He descended to the dead.
    On the third day he rose again.
    He ascended into heaven,
        and is seated at the right hand of the Father.
    He will come again to judge the living and the dead.

I believe in the Holy Spirit,
    the holy catholic Church,
    the communion of saints,
    the forgiveness of sins,
    the resurrection of the body,
    and the life everlasting. Amen.

or

II. THE APOSTLES' CREED

I believe in God, the Father almighty,
    maker of heaven and earth;

And in Jesus Christ, his only Son, our Lord;
    who was conceived by the Holy Ghost,
    born of the Virgin Mary,
    suffered under Pontius Pilate,
    was crucified, dead, and buried.
    He descended into hell.
    The third day he rose again from the dead.
    He ascended into heaven,
    and sitteth on the right hand of God the Father almighty.
    From thence he shall come to judge the quick and the dead.

I believe in the Holy Ghost,
    the holy catholic Church,
    the communion of saints,
    the forgiveness of sins,
    the resurrection of the body,
    and the life everlasting. Amen.

N.B. A metrical version of the creed may be sung using RIL, hymn 609.

N. _____ *(use Christian names, omit surname)*

do you believe in your heart that you are called by God's Church, and therefore by God, to be a minister of the Gospel of Jesus Christ?

I do so believe.

Do you believe the books of the Old and New Testaments to be the Word of God and the perfect doctrine of salvation; rejecting all doctrines contrary thereto?

I do so believe.

Will you proclaim the Gospel of our Lord and Savior Jesus Christ; will you from the Word of God instruct, admonish, comfort, and reprove, according to everyone's need; and uphold the witness of holy Scripture against all schisms and heresies?

I will, the Lord being my helper.

Will you call upon the name of the Lord for and with the whole congregation; administer the sacraments according to his command; share responsibility for the mutual Christian growth of all members of the congregation; and exercise Christian love and discipline?

I will, the Lord being my helper.

Will you be loyal to the witness and work of the Reformed Church in America, accepting its order and discipline, using all your abilities to further its Christian mission, here and throughout the world?

I will, the Lord being my helper.

ORDINATION

The candidate shall then kneel. The presiding officer shall ask the ministers of classis to come forward. Those the classis shall invite may join in the laying on of hands. The presiding officer shall say:

The Lord Jesus prayed on behalf of his disciples: "Holy Father, keep them in your name which you have given me, that they may be one, even as we are one. Sanctify them in the truth; your word is truth. As you did send me into the world, so I have sent them into the world. And for their sake I consecrate myself, that they also may be consecrated in truth." *John 17:11, 17-19*

Let us pray. Almighty God, who through Jesus Christ calls from among us those who carry out the ministry of the Word, enlighten your servant with your Spirit, strengthen *him   her* with your hand; and so govern *him   her* that *his   her* life and labor may be to the glory of your name and the advancement of your kingdom, through Jesus Christ our Lord. **Amen.**

The presiding officer shall say to the candidate:

N._____ *(use Christian names, omit surname)*

by the authority given to his Church by our Lord Jesus Christ, we ordain you minister of the Word, in the name of the Father and of the Son and of the Holy Spirit. The Lord bless you and keep you: The Lord make his face to shine upon you and be gracious to you: The Lord lift up the light of his countenance upon you and give you peace. The grace of our Lord Jesus Christ will be with you always. **Amen.**

ORATION AND SIGNING OF THE FORM OF DECLARATION

The candidate, having received ordination, shall stand and read aloud the "Form of the Declaration for Ministers" and sign the book containing the declaration. If a symbol of the ministry (such as a Bible or pulpit robe) is to be presented, it should be given at this time. Those who participate in the laying on of hands shall extend the right hand of fellowship before returning to their places with the members of classis. The candidate shall remain standing for the charge.

CHARGE TO THE MINISTER

The person designated by the classis shall deliver the charge. The charge which follows shall be read, but an additional brief exhortation, if authorized by the classis, may be made before it.

Beloved fellow servant in Christ, be attentive to the flock whom the Holy Spirit may give you to shepherd and teach, and to all those among whom you shall labor. Love Christ, and feed his sheep. "For to this end we toil and strive, because we have our hope set on the living God, who is the Savior of all—especially of those who believe. Command and teach those things. Set the believers an example in speech and conduct, in love, in faith, in purity. Attend to the public reading of Scripture, to preaching, to teaching. Do not neglect the gift you have. Practice these duties, devote yourself to them."

I Timothy 4:10-15

In the presence of God who gives life to all things, and of Christ Jesus who in his testimony before Pontius Pilate made the good confession, I charge you to keep the commandment unstained and free from reproach until the appearing of the Lord Jesus Christ; and this will be made manifest at the proper time by the blessed and only Sovereign, the King of kings and Lord of lords, who alone has immortality and dwells in unapproachable light, whom no man has ever seen or can see. To him be honor and eternal dominion. **Amen.**

I Timothy 6:13-16

If the service is also one of installation, omit the following indented material.
The presiding officer shall say:

PRAYER FOR GRACE

Let us pray.

The prayer may be spoken by the whole congregation.

Most merciful God, we thank you for the service you call us to render within the Church of Christ, and for the commission to proclaim the gospel to all the world. We ask you continually to strengthen N. _____

(use Christian names, omit surname)

by your Holy Spirit, for the ministry to which you have chosen and called *him* **her. Enlighten** *his* **her understanding, endow** *him* **her with wisdom and courage, speak to**

him   her   **that**   *he   she*   **may boldly make known the gospel. Grant**
him   her   **the grace to savor the joys of ministry in Christ's name**
along with the patience to bear the difficulties and trials which may
come, that being sustained by your spirit   *he   she*   **may remain**
steadfast, always rejoicing in the words of our Lord, who promised
his disciples, "I am with you always, to the close of the age."

*For a service of ordination only there may follow the GENERAL PRAYERS, and
the LORD'S PRAYER, unless it has been used already in the service. A HYMN
of Thanksgiving may be sung after which the newly ordained minister shall deliver
the BENEDICTION.*

INSTALLATION

*The classis may authorize the presiding officer or other designated person to
deliver a brief EXHORTATION TO THE CONGREGATION after which
the presiding officer shall say:*

AFFIRMATION BY THE CONGREGATION

Will all those within the fellowship of _____ *(name of the church)*
rise and make their affirmation of the minister whom God has given them?

When the members of the congregation have risen, the presiding officer shall continue:

Beloved in the Lord Jesus Christ, do you receive in the name of the Lord,
this his servant N. _____ *(use Christian names, omit surname)*
to be your pastor and teacher?

In the Lord's name we receive   *him   her*   **and make this pledge: To receive**
with meekness and love the word of truth   *he   she*   **proclaims, and to**
submit with confidence and good cheer to the pastoral care   *he   she*
provides in Christ's service. We promise and pledge our encouragement and
prayers, our participation and labor, as together we do the work of the
Church. We promise that we will furnish   *him   her*   **such financial and**
personal care as will enable   *him   her*   **to do**   *his   her*   **work joyfully and**
productively, as long as our pastoral relationship continues.

The Lord bless you and pour out his Spirit to strengthen you, that you may
keep these vows in the name of Christ and to his glory. **Amen.**

DECLARATION

The people and the candidate may be seated. The presiding officers shall then say:

In the name and by the authority of the Classis of _____
_____ I now declare that the pastoral relationship
between the Reverend _____ *(using full name)* and the _____
_____ *(name of church)* is fully constituted, and that the Reverend
_____ *(using full name)* is the lawfully installed pastor and teacher of
this church.

PRAYER FOR GRACE

Let us pray.

The prayer may be spoken by the whole congregation.

Most merciful God, we thank you for the service you call us to render within the Church of Christ, and for the commission to proclaim the gospel to all the world. We ask you continually to strengthen N._____ *(use Christian names, omit surname)* by your Holy Spirit, for the ministry to which you have chosen and called *him her.* Enlighten *his her* understanding, endow *him her* with wisdom and courage, speak to *him her* that *he she* may boldly make known the gospel. Grant *him her* the grace to savor the joys of ministry in Christ's name along with the patience to bear the difficulties and trials which may come, that being sustained by your spirit, *he she* may remain steadfast, always rejoicing in the words of the Lord, who promised his disciples, "I am with you always, to the close of the age."

Then may follow the GENERAL PRAYERS, and the LORD'S PRAYER, unless it has been used already in the service. A HYMN of Thanksgiving may be sung after which the newly ordained and installed minister shall deliver the BENEDICTION.

RECEPTION INTO THE CLASSIS AND INSTALLATION OF A MINISTER OF THE WORD

The Book of Church Order (Part I, Article 2, Section 2) directs that, after a call to a minister of the Word to the pastorate of a church has been approved by the classis and accepted by the minister, the name of the person so called "shall be published in the church on three successive Sundays, so that opportunity may be afforded for the raising of lawful objections." There being none, the Book of Church Order further directs (Part II, Article 10, Sections 2 and 5) that the classis shall install the minister of the Word into his/her office.

This order is intended for use when a minister of the Word is to be installed as pastor and teacher of a congregation. Installation into other appropriate ministries should be conducted in accordance with the DIRECTORY FOR THE RECEPTION INTO THE CLASSIS AND INSTALLATION INTO A SPECIALIZED MINISTRY.

After the Approach to God and a proclamation of The Word of God in Scripture reading and sermon, the presiding officer of classis shall begin:

PRAYER

Let us pray.

O God, the great shepherd of the church, who through the light of your Holy Spirit has always guided your people: grant that we, by the same Spirit, may live for you, and together with all whom you call to serve within the body of Christ, may be faithful and obedient to your Word, through Jesus Christ our Lord. **Amen.**

EXPOSITION

Beloved in the Lord, Holy Scripture teaches us that God our heavenly Father gathers to himself from among the lost children of this world a Church to life eternal, and that in this work of grace he is pleased to use our ministry. The Lord Jesus himself provides us with the grace we need to serve him, as affirmed by the Apostle Paul: "and his gifts were that some should be apostles, some prophets, some evangelists, some pastors and teachers, to equip the saints for the work of ministry, for building up the body of Christ."

Ephesians 4:11-12

RECEPTION INTO THE CLASSIS

PRESENTATION AND INTERROGATION OF THE CANDIDATE

The presiding officer shall say:

Will the Reverend _____ *(using full name)* now rise and stand before the classis and this congregation.

When the candidate has done so, the presiding officer continues:

N. _____ *(use Christian names, omit surname)* , the Classis of

_____has approved
the Call issued to you by the _____ Church of
_____ to be their pastor and teacher. You stand before us now
in order that you may be received into the membership of the classis and
installed into the new ministry to which you have been called. So that it may
be clear to all here present that you are both willing and able to exercise the
ministry of the Word within the Church of Christ, I call upon you to reaffirm
the vows made when you were ordained a minister of the Word: Do you
believe in your heart that you are called by God's church, and therefore by
God, to be a minister of the Gospel of Jesus Christ?

I do so believe.

Do you believe the books of the Old and New Testaments to be the Word of
God and the perfect doctrine of salvation; rejecting all doctrines contrary
thereto?

I do so believe.

Will you proclaim the Gospel of our Lord and Savior Jesus Christ; will you
from the Word of God instruct, admonish, comfort, and reprove, according
to everyone's need; and uphold the witness of holy Scripture against all schisms
and heresies?

I will, the Lord being my helper.

Will you call upon the name of the Lord for and with the whole congregation;
administer the sacraments according to his command; share responsibility for
the mutual Christian growth of all members of the congregation; and exercise
Christian love and discipline?

I will, the Lord being my helper.

Will you be loyal to the witness and work of the Reformed Church in America, accepting its order and discipline, using all your abilities to further its
Christian mission, here and throughout the world?

I will, the Lord being my helper.

Will you declare all these things publicly and make your commitment to a
Christian ministry among us?

> *The Candidate shall respond by reading aloud the* "Form of the Declaration for
> Ministers" *after which he/she shall sign the book containing the declaration.*

WELCOME

> *The presiding officer shall welcome the candidate using these words or some other
> suitable greeting after which he/she and such other officers or members of the classis
> as may have been appointed may extend the right hand of fellowship to the new
> member.*

In the name of the Lord Jesus Christ, the Head of the Church, we welcome
you into our fellowship and pledge to you our confidence, support, and affection as you live and work among us as a fellow servant and minister of the
Word of God.

INSTALLATION

STATEMENT ON THE CONGREGATION'S MINISTRY

The new member and other members of classis may return to their places, after which the presiding officer or an elder from the calling congregation appointed by him/her may make a brief STATEMENT *regarding the nature and/or heritage of the congregation so as to reveal something of the direction in which God may be calling it to go during the future, after which the presiding officer shall ask the candidate to stand before the body and inquire:*

ACCEPTANCE BY THE MINISTER

In accepting the call issued by the _____ Church of _____ , you have already acknowledged your willingness to serve God as their pastor and teacher. Do you now affirm publicly your acceptance of that office?

I do.

The candidate may make a further brief statement in his/her own words, facing and addressing both classis and congregation.

ACCEPTANCE BY THE CONGREGATION

The presiding officer shall call upon the congregation to rise:

Will all those within the fellowship of _____ *(name of church)* rise and make their affirmation of the minister whom God has given them?

When the members of the congregation have risen, the presiding officer shall continue:

Beloved in the Lord Jesus Christ, do you receive in the name of the Lord, this his servant N. _____ *(use Christian names, omit surname)* to be your pastor and teacher?

In the Lord's name we receive *him* *her***, and make this pledge: to receive with meekness and love the word of truth** *he* *she* **proclaims, and to submit with confidence and good cheer to the pastoral care** *he* *she* **provides in Christ's service. We promise and pledge our encouragement and prayers, our participation and labor, as together we do the work of the Church. We promise that we will furnish** *him* *her* **such financial and personal support as will enable** *him* *her* **to do** *his* *her* **work joyfully and productively, as long as our pastoral relationship continues.**

The Lord bless you and pour out his Spirit to strengthen you, that you may keep these vows in the name of Christ and to his glory. **Amen.**

Brief, scriptural charges may be made to the minister-elect and the congregation. The presiding officer shall then declare:

DECLARATION OF INSTALLATION

In the name and by the authority of the Classis of _____ , I now declare that the pastoral relationship between the Reverend _____ _____ *(using full name)* and the _____ *(name of church)* is fully constituted, and the Reverend _____ *(using full name)* is the lawfully installed pastor and teacher of this church. Let us call upon the name of the Lord.

PRAYER FOR GRACE

Let us pray.

Most merciful God, we thank you for the service you call us to render within the Church of Christ and for the commission to proclaim the gospel to all the world. We ask you to continually strengthen N. _____

_____(use Christian names, omit surname)_by your Holy Spirit for the ministry to which you have chosen and called *him   her*. Enlighten *his   her* understanding; endow *him   her* with wisdom and courage; speak to *him   her* that *he   she* may boldly make known the gospel. Grant *him   her* the grace to savor the joys of ministry in Christ's name along with the patience to bear the difficulties and trials which may come, that being sustained by your Spirit, *he   she* may remain steadfast, always rejoicing in the words of the Lord, who promised his disciples, "I am with you always, to the close of the age."

Give your grace also to this congregation, set apart for the ministry that becomes God's people. Strengthen them as they work together in your Church; enlighten them through the proclamation of your Word so that they may be indeed what you called them to be through the Apostle Peter: "...a chosen race, a royal priesthood, a holy nation, God's own people, that you may declare the wonderful deeds of him who called you out of darkness into his marvelous light." **Amen.**

> *Then may follow the* GENERAL PRAYERS *and the* LORD'S PRAYER, *unless it has been used already in the service. A* HYMN *of thanksgiving may be sung after which the newly installed minister shall deliver the:*

BENEDICTION

DIRECTORY FOR RECEPTION INTO THE CLASSIS AND INSTALLATION INTO A SPECIALIZED MINISTRY

The classis shall appoint a time for a service of worship during which praise and prayer shall be offered, the Word of God read and a sermon preached, after which the Order specified below shall take place.

PRAYER: The presiding officer of classis or a person designated by the officer shall lead the congregation in a prayer asking for God's blessing upon the assembly.

EXPOSITION: The presiding officer shall give a brief exposition of the divine call to ministry, using the text Ephesians 4:11-12 or another appropriate portion of Scripture.

PRESENTATION OF THE CANDIDATE: The presiding officer shall call the candidate to stand before the congregation for the purpose of being received into the classis (if he/she is not already a member) and being installed into his/her office.

INTERROGATION: The presiding officer shall ask the candidate to reaffirm his/her ordination vows. After receiving a positive oral response, the presiding officer shall ask the candidate if he/she is willing to declare his/her faith publicly and make a renewed commitment to perform a Christian ministry as a member of the classis.

READING AND SIGNING OF THE FORM OF DECLARATION: The candidate shall reply to the presiding officer's questions by reading the *Form of the Declaration for Ministers* and affixing his/her name to a book containing the declaration.

WELCOME: The presiding officer and such other officers or members of the classis as may be appointed shall welcome the candidate as a minister member of the classis with a greeting and the extending of the right hand of fellowship.

STATEMENT OF THE NATURE OF THE MINISTRY: A brief statement regarding the nature of the particular ministry and the duties pertaining to it which the minister may be called upon to perform may be read by the presiding officer, or by a person appointed to do so, after which the following affirmations shall be made.

ACCEPTANCE OF THE OFFICE BY THE CANDIDATE: The president shall ask the minister if he/she is willing to affirm publicly his/her acceptance of the office. The minister shall make a brief reply using his/her own words.

ACCEPTANCE OF THE CANDIDATE: If there are persons present who will be taking an active role in this ministry, the presiding officer shall ask them to stand to affirm their willingness to accept the minister God has given them and to participate in ministry with *him/her* as God may lead them.

If the ministry is under the direct supervision of the classis or its committee(s), or if the classis is acting on behalf of another assembly of the Reformed Church in America, its members shall stand with, or in place of, the group present and join in the affirmation.

CHARGES: Brief, scriptural charges may be made to the minister-elect and, if present, to those participating in the ministry.

DECLARATION OF INSTALLATION: The presiding officer shall make a declaration using this form: "In the name and by the authority of the Classis of _____ , I declare that the Reverend _____ _____ *(using full name)* is duly installed _____ *(into the particular ministry)*."

PRAYERS: A prayer for grace may be offered and the general prayers made, concluding with the Lord's Prayer unless it has been used previously in the service.

BENEDICTION: The newly installed minister may pronounce the blessing concluding the service.

NOTE: Appropriate HYMNS may be sung during the Order, if desired. It is suggested that these be included before the *Statement of the Nature of the Ministry* and/or before the *Benediction*.

PART IV
The Directory
for Worship

WORSHIP

Worship is the action of acknowledging God's worth! Penitence, forgiveness, joy, a growth in Christian knowledge—all may and should happen while at worship, but all are results of the central meaning and action of worship: the acknowledgment of God's worth.

The words of the Bible in both Hebrew and Greek which are translated "worship" are all verbs describing the action (by bowing, prostrating oneself, or kissing the hand) of acknowledging another of greater worth. From votum to benediction, our worship is both a dialogue between minister and congregation and between God and people. It is the sung, verbal, and acted expressions of adoration, confession, forgiveness; the reception of grace in Word and Sacrament; and response in acknowledging God's worth.

God has initiated a self-revelation of his worth to Israel and in Christ, recorded for us in Holy Scripture, which reveals the God of justice/grace, a God who would have us live in covenant relationship with him.

When worship is the acknowledgment of God's worth, then penitence, forgiveness, joy, a growth in Christian knowledge—all these things will be added unto us. Even as the liturgy is a paradigm of the Christian life, so worship images the meaning of that life. Worship is losing oneself during the encounter with God's greatness. In finding this truth, everything else in worship and in life shall be added unto it: "For whoever would save his life will lose it; and whoever loses his life for my sake, he will save it" *Luke 9:24*.

THE SOURCE OF WORSHIP

The Triune God reveals himself in the history of Israel and in Jesus Christ, and this revelation is authoritatively set forth in the pages of Holy Scripture as the Holy Spirit opens our hearts in the experience of God's worth.

The history of Israel's worship, together with its fulfillment in Christ and the experience of the early church, provides us with the *STRUCTURE* of worship.

We proclaim what the Bible tells us about God's worth: that he creates all things good; that when we sinned, God sent his only Son that we might have life; and that through the Holy Spirit God confirms us in that life. This is true worth.

REALITY

Worship is not only the expression of piety but deals with the whole of life. Worship deals with reality; it encompasses the entire week. At the heart of the reality of worship is the worth of God, and we acknowledge that worth in action: in congregational amens, hymns, dialogue in Scripture (whether in sentences or psalm), prayers of confession, reception of the Word in forgiveness and hope, confession of faith, the peace, participation in the sacraments, the giving of our gifts in thanksgiving, prayers, and silence. Where the structure of the service enables this action to take place smoothly and naturally, it is a guide to the reality of faith. Worship enables believers to articulate faith and to act it out in word, song, and gesture. In the reality of worship these actions lead toward the living of Christianity all through the week. The ritual, or action, of worship is important because it is the pattern for life.

Because worship deals with reality, it has structure, for we are called by God to praise him, acknowledge our sin, experience grace, and go forth to live in gratitude. As God encounters us in many ways, so there may be variety in the response of worship, but because it serves as a corporate model for Christian life, it also has structure and sequence.

Corporate worship reflects God's worth in the reality of our calling to be members of the Body of Christ. Because we are all members of the one body, we come together on the Lord's day to worship as one.

Section II:
STRUCTURE: APPROACH, WORD IN PROCLAMATION AND SACRAMENT, RESPONSE

Worship in the Old Testament was centered in the temple with its ritual of sacrificial atonement, and later in the synagogue and its service of the Word. In the New Testament, Jesus Christ becomes the once-for-all sacrifice for the church so that in worship the liturgy of the Lord's Supper becomes the fulfillment of the sacrifice of the temple. The service of the Word is in continuity with the synagogue service; the service of the Lord's Supper celebrates the distinctive fulfillment of the Old Covenant in the New Covenant of Christ's Body and Blood, thus embracing the fullness of God's revelation.

The service of grace, *WORD IN PROCLAMATION AND SACRAMENT*, exists within the structure of *APPROACH* and *RESPONSE*. This pattern is present throughout the Bible; the whole story of the Exodus; the illustration of Isaiah 6; the numerous miracles in the Gospel narratives—all have in common an approach wherein God and people confront each other. God is made known in Word and Act, and the people respond to God's presence. This same structure of biblical experience is reflected in the Heidelberg Catechism as a living reflection of biblical truth. The catechism is divided into sections on guilt, grace, and gratitude, as is the structure of worship: *APPROACH, WORD IN PROCLAMATION AND SACRAMENT*, and *RESPONSE*. The Heidelberg opens with a hymn of confidence before going on to the confession of guilt; so too in the *APPROACH* one sings adoration to God before confession and forgiveness. After bringing us to a recognition of our need for a Savior, the Heidelberg Catechism sets forth the means of God's grace through Word and Sacrament. Both proclamation and sacramental action are the means of God's grace; both indicate his initiative in coming to save us in the Word, Jesus Christ.

Gratitude is the response called for by the catechism. The model of law and the Lord's Prayer are a means of guiding us in lives of thankfulness in response to God's grace. Similarly, in the liturgy *WORD IN PROCLAMATION AND SACRAMENT* is answered by the thanksgiving of obedience and prayer.

As it is a model for life, it is fitting that the liturgy end with the RESPONSE, which can be articulated in the lives of the worshipers throughout the week:

lives that are forgiving even as they have been forgiven; lives in which the worth of God shines forth in God-like ways as love and compassion are given without a demand for reciprocity; lives which seek good for others and show thankfulness in their daily dispositions.

WORD IN PROCLAMATION AND SACRAMENT characterizes the heart of the liturgy and furnishes content and structure. Within the context of PROCLAMATION AND SACRAMENT, we have freedom in the structure of worship even as we are allowed freedom within the structure of our lives. We may have freedom in worship as long as the biblical lessons control the structure for our worship. Our freedom is governed by the proclaimed Word. The lections determine the liturgy.

The elements are discussed in Section III in a sequence which has been normative, though an understanding of the structure and sequence of worship allows a great deal of flexibility.

Worship is the action of acknowledging God's worth. Its essential structure is the APPROACH; God's grace given through the WORD IN PROCLAMATION AND SACRAMENT; and our RESPONSE. Worship involves minister and congregation in a coherent dialogical sequence of action.

Adhering to the above, there are opportunities for many variables in worship: a service of WORD IN PROCLAMATION AND SACRAMENT within a restricted length of time could begin with a votum and the preparatory service; followed by the scripture lessons and sermon; followed by the creed, the peace, offertory and Lord's Supper; followed by a response of the communion thanksgiving and benediction. Hymns could be sung while the elements were being served rather than where otherwise placed, thereby allowing a brief but complete service.

Another example of freedom concerns the Sacrament of Baptism. While the normative location for the Sacrament of Baptism is in the section on WORD IN PROCLAMATION AND SACRAMENT, it is also appropriate to celebrate baptism within the APPROACH to God by virtue of its content as confession, cleansing, and incorporation into the Body of Christ.

Section III:
THE ELEMENTS OF WORSHIP

THE APPROACH TO GOD

VOTUM

The Votum begins worship by announcing who God is and who we are: "Our help is in the name of the Lord, who made heaven and earth" (Psalm 124:8). Votum is a Latin word, meaning desire, which in the Middle Ages was applied to a layperson whose desire (votum) was to serve Christ with an intensity equal to that of those who had entered the monastery. Later it was used of the monastic vow. Thus the use of this term, Votum, as the opening statement of reformed worship is to express the desire that our whole life, represented in this worship, is ever lived in the acknowledgment of God's help, and only his help, in heaven and on earth. The people will affirm this, their desire, with a vocal "Amen."

SENTENCES

The Sentences present an opportunity for the liturgist to set the tone or direction for worship. While the Sentences may be drawn from many places in Scripture, the Psalms run the full gamut of religious feeling, written with a beauty befitting the content of their religious expression.

The Sentences offer an opportunity to involve the congregation in worship in a very active way. The biblical truth about worship as the action of the people of God can be immediately demonstrated by having the people read the word of Scripture responsively. This is not a new idea, but is as old as the Psalms themselves, many of which were sung antiphonally as the people approached the temple.

The lessons of the lectionary offer a rich treasure for appropriate sentences.

SALUTATION

The Salutation is the greeting by which Christ reminds us that he is in our midst, bringing grace, mercy, and peace. Ordinarily the Salutation will come from the Epistles. If an Old Testament greeting is used, a Christological or Trinitarian declaration should be added.

Since the Salutation conveys to the worshiper God's great gift of grace, mercy, and peace, bought for us by the precious blood of Christ, colloquial substitutes like "hello" or "good morning" are both inadequate and inappropriate.

Because greeting the congregation on behalf of Christ is a great privilege, the minister should deliver this greeting so that love and joy may be felt by all present.

HYMN

The greeting by Christ is immediately followed by the congregation's outburst of praise in a hymn. This hymn is an expression of joy that God is in our midst; we acknowledge God's worth as the almighty, merciful, loving, and sustaining Lord. Throughout the history of the church, hymnody has been perceived as prayer, and in the words of Augustine, "those who sing, pray twice."

CONFESSION, ASSURANCE OF PARDON, AND LAW

The worshiper who rejoices in God's presence is confronted and judged by that presence. Worship is the acknowledgment of God's superior worth: God is righteous, we are unrighteous; God is sinless, we are sinners.

PRAYER OF CONFESSION

In the prayer of confession we acknowledge that we are sinners. The corporate nature of the prayer reflects the truth that sin is not only individual, but shared by humanity. Sin is both individual and corporate. To deny either allows self-righteousness. The prayer, prayed corporately, helps the congregation to recognize that in buying and selling, in peace and in war, we are inextricably a part of the inequality and exploitation of this world, and that we must face the truth about ourselves and our need continually to ask forgiveness. The corporate prayer may well allow a period of silence in which we confess our involvement in corporate sin, as well as individual sins.

KYRIE ELEISON (LORD HAVE MERCY)

The Kyrie is such a permanent fixture among Orthodox, Roman Catholics, and Protestants that it retains its New Testament Greek name. While its usage has varied, its Greek title is a reminder that all of Christendom includes this prayer as an integral part of its worship.

ASSURANCE OF PARDON

The truth stated liturgically in the Assurance of Pardon is the same as that of John 3:16—"For God so loved the world that he gave his only Son, that whoever believes in him should not perish but have eternal life." It is Christ who forgives, by his incarnation, atoning death, and victory in the resurrection. Since the minister is God's mouth, words of forgiveness have the full weight of biblical authority.

For this awesome task it befits the humility of the minister to use the words of Scripture for the absolution. The person seeking forgiveness needs to hear the full authority of Christ's Word. Therefore, the minister is to pronounce authoritatively Christ's truth with joy and certainty.

Appropriate scriptural declarations of forgiveness may be used in all of their biblical variety.

THE LAW OF GOD

The use of the Law in this sequence of confession, forgiveness, and law is a contribution of the reformed churches to Christendom. This is known as Calvin's third use of the law: as a guide to Christian living. It is part of the Heidelberg Catechism's structure of guilt, grace, and gratitude. Law is explained not in the section on guilt, but in the section on gratitude. From the perspective of judgment, the law has been fulfilled in Christ. In union with him Christians live in gratitude, in covenant relationship, and in obedience to God's law.

While the Ten Commandments are read frequently at this point, the worship leader is free to use the law as it is found throughout Scripture.

PRAISE: PSALTER AND GLORIA PATRI, HYMN, OR ANTHEM

Having encapsulated the Christian life in the liturgical sequence of confession, forgiveness, and law, the natural response of the Christian is praise. We praise God by Psalter, hymn, or anthem.

The Psalter, the oldest book of songs for the people of God, is most appropriate as a means of praise. In many churches the Psalter lesson for the day is read responsively at this point. As a response of joy, the Psalm should be read with alacrity, that the flow of praise may not be slowed or broken. The Psalm should be followed with its Christian attachment, a doxology—frequently the Gloria Patri. Because the church has attached the Gloria Patri to the Psalm to articulate its Christian perception of the Psalms, the congregation should stand for both Psalm and Gloria Patri.

There is also the opportunity to sing the Psalm, for many of the Psalms are to be found in our hymnals and may appropriately be sung at this point.

If there is a hymn that is appropriate to conclude the sequence of confession, forgiveness, and law, it may be used instead of a Psalm and the Gloria Patri.

Praise has been so much a part of the worship of the church that the resources are many. The choir, as representatives of the congregation, may lead in an appropriate anthem which could take the place of Psalter (said or sung) or hymn.

THE WORD OF GOD IN PROCLAMATION AND SACRAMENT

The Word in Proclamation

The congregation is enabled to grow in their worship of God who is revealed in the Word. Accordingly, the Word of God is read and then made understandable and applicable to our age. God speaks to the congregation through the mouth of the minister, and through the Spirit opens the ears of his people.

PRAYER FOR ILLUMINATION

The proclamation of the Word begins with a petition entreating God to kindle the light of faith which enables the Word to come alive in us.

LESSONS

Lectionary

The full counsel of God shines through clearly when a lectionary is used to determine the Scriptures to be read and preached.

Lectionaries were developed with a concern for the entire Bible, for the liturgical year, and for the persons and work of the Trinity. The best minds of the church sought to exercise the teaching office by offering a guide to parish ministers, that the Holy Scripture in its fullness might be read to the congregation.

The lectionary has several advantages: 1) it covers a great breadth of Scripture—the whole counsel of God, helping guard the minister from tarrying too long in a favorite book or subject; 2) while providing a sequence from week to week (usually from the Gospel), 3) it also relates the Gospel to its Old Testament antecedents (including an appropriate Psalter passage) and frequently to a lesson from the Epistles; 4) it follows the Christian year with its focus upon Christ; 5) it speaks to the persons and work of the Trinity; and 6) it protects the congregation from the possibility of a narrow preoccupation with the New Testament to the exclusion of the Old.

Lectio Continua

Meaning a "continuous reading," the term has been used ever since the Reformation to describe preaching through a book of the Bible from beginning to end.

The advantage of this method is that it enables the preacher to treat the book as the whole that it was meant to be. It further enables the preacher to focus study on a book of the Bible with more thoroughness than might otherwise be possible, and enables the congregation to learn the message of an entire book of Scripture.

Ministers responsible for a morning and evening sermon each Sunday will almost certainly wish to prepare one of their sermons on the basis of *lectio continua*.

Heidelberg Catechism

The *Book of Church Order* of the Reformed Church in America requires that all the points of doctrine of the Heidelberg Catechism be preached every four years. Although the ecumenical lectionaries cover the points of doctrine, those who wish to follow the sequence of the Catechism may refer to the *Liturgy and Psalms*, 1968, which has a lectionary for such catechetical preaching. Its advantage is that it offers the congregation a structure of theology and a familiarity with one of the finest of our confessions of faith.

SERMON

Preaching is the proclamation of the message of Scripture. Whether or not the preacher focuses upon the message of the sequential lesson or whether the preaching includes all of the lections will depend in part upon the content of the passages and the needs of the congregation, and the style and intent of the proclaimer. Preaching is an opportunity to speak God's worth to the church. As such, it is both a part of worship and the occasion for worship. Within the context of worship, the primary emphasis of preaching must be upon God's worth.

Preaching within worship is the setting forth of God's worth, so that we, in gratitude, may seek to be like God. The relevance of such proclamation lies in communicating how God's worth is to be reflected in our lives. A minister who preaches that the congregation may worship God in Word and life must show how a God-like life is lived in our day.

PRAYER FOR BLESSING

A prayer shall be offered as a thanksgiving for the truth revealed in the Word and as a supplication that this truth may be further revealed in our lives.

> *When worship includes only the grace of the* WORD IN PROCLAMATION, *then the creed, offering, doxology, prayers of thanksgiving and intercession, hymn, and benediction may be understood as the congregation's* RESPONSE *to God's Word.*

CONFESSION OF FAITH

Having approached God in praise and confession, and having heard the word of grace, the congregation now responds in the affirmation of their belief through the creed.

The Apostles' or Nicene Creed will perhaps be most frequently confessed as a summary of our Christian faith. However, the extensive treasures of confessional statements which enrich our Reformed Church should not be overlooked. The Scriptures and doctrinal standards (the ecumenical creeds, the Belgic Confession, the Heidelberg Catechism, and the Canons of Dort), together with *Our Song of Hope*, which includes provisions for singing, may all be used for purposes of confession of faith.

The confession of faith is always to be made by the congregation and never by the minister alone, because it is the response of the congregation to the proclamation of God's Word of Grace.

PEACE

As a token of our reconciliation with one another, the congregation exchanges the Peace. Even as Jesus commanded, we are not to celebrate our reconciliation with God unless in our lives we have been reconciled with one another and witness that we are members of one body.

The Peace may be shared through words, a smile, a handshake, a kiss, an embrace, or any other gesture that is appropriate within the social context of the congregation.

When the Sacrament is celebrated, this is the historic position for the Peace. When the Sacrament is not celebrated, theological warrant could be made for the Peace after the Confession of Sin, or at the end of the service of the WORD IN PROCLAMATION.

OFFERING

In the early church, the offering marked the bringing of the food for the celebration of the Lord's Supper. After the Supper had been celebrated in the church, the remaining food was taken by the deacons to be distributed among the poor of the congregation.

When in some churches it became customary not to celebrate the Lord's Supper each Sunday, an offering of money was received at this time, some of which was used to assist the poor.

Today, after the offering of money has been received from the congregation, these gifts, together with the bread and wine for the Eucharist, are to be brought to the front of the church. The elements are placed on the Lord's Table for celebration, and the monetary offerings are put in another appropriate place.

DOXOLOGY

When the bread and wine of the sacrament are carried forward, together with the offerings of the people, the congregation rises to praise God in the familiar words of the Doxology. To its familiar meaning of extolling God for temporal blessings, from which we return a portion to him, is added in the eucharistic context the praise of thanksgiving for the gift of Jesus Christ which we are about to celebrate in the Lord's Supper.

The Word in the Sacrament of the Lord's Supper

MEANING OF THE SACRAMENT

When the Eucharist is celebrated frequently, it may be desirable to use a brief and felicitous description of the meaning of the sacrament which emphasizes remembrance, communion, and hope. The remembrance is of our Lord's passion on the cross and the resulting forgiveness of our sin; our communion is with our resurrected Lord Jesus Christ and the other members of that living body; and our hope is that as surely as we eat this bread and drink this wine, we will as surely be raised from the dead unto everlasting life, since Christ in his ascension promises that he will come again to make all things new.

INVITATION

An invitation to participate in the sacrament is extended to communicants by the minister in the name of Christ, who is the host at his table. It shall be extended also to those communicants who are not members of the particular congregation.

COMMUNION PRAYER

A prayer shall be offered which includes thanksgiving to God for his creative work, providence, and revelation, especially in Christ. This prayer is usually punctuated by the acclamation of the people to Christ in the words of the Sanctus (Rev. 4:8b), and by their hosannas (John 12:13). This exclamation, which brings the historical past of the incarnate life of Christ together with the eschatological future, is entirely appropriate to the celebration of the Supper, which does the same. The short period of silence which follows reflects the description of worship in the book of Revelation, where after the adoration of God all of heaven keeps silence.

The Communion prayer continues with: thanksgiving to God for his work of redemption by the recalling of the birth, life, suffering, death, and resurrection of Jesus Christ and the gift of the Holy Spirit; the offering of ourselves in Christ as holy and living sacrifices; a petition for the working of the Holy Spirit among us so that the breaking of bread and the sharing of the cup will be to us the communion of the Body and Blood of Christ; a petition for the unity of Christ's body, the church, which is affirmed in the celebration of the Supper; and in conclusion a thanksgiving for our hope in Christ, with the frequent addition of the ancient prayer of Scripture: Maranatha, "Come, Lord Jesus."

COMMUNION

In communion the words of institution remain always the same, those Jesus spoke to his disciples in the Upper Room. Whether the blessing over the bread is separated from the blessing of the cup will depend largely on how the sacrament is distributed in a given congregation. For example, during the first meal in the Upper Room, the blessing of the bread began the meal, while the blessing of the cup probably came at the very end when the cup of wine was shared.

When the congregation remains in the pew, the bread will be distributed immediately after the words of institution for the bread have been spoken. In an attempt to give some sense of unity, many congregations retain the bread and all eat at once when the minister recites the words for distribution (1 Cor. 10:16). Then in a separate gesture the words of institution for the cup are read, and again people retain their glasses until all have been served and the minister recites "the cup of blessing which we bless is the communion of the blood of Christ."

In congregations where the communicants come forward to sit or stand about a table, the words of institution for both bread and wine will be said consecutively, and the bread and wine will follow one another around the communion table. In such instances, if the congregation serves one another, they will frequently follow the minister's example by saying, "the bread which we break is the communion of the Body of Christ," with the corresponding phrase for the wine.

THE RESPONSE TO GOD

THANKSGIVING AFTER COMMUNION

Having heard and tasted God's grace in the proclaimed Word and visible Word of bread and wine, the congregation responds with a biblical Psalm of Thanksgiving. It should always be an occasion of celebration and ought to be entered into with joy by minister and congregation.

INTERCESSION

Intercessory prayers express our gratitude for God's gifts and our participation in the communion of the saints as we offer our concern for the world in the name of Christ. The intercessions may be concluded with the Lord's Prayer. The prayers of intercession are also a place where churches which practice healing may appropriately engage in that service within the liturgy. In this connection the laying on of hands and anointing with oil may also be practiced.

HYMN

Time permitting, if hymns have not been sung during the distribution of the elements of the Lord's Supper, it is appropriate to close the service with a final hymn of praise, either rejoicing in our Lord's resurrection or in his coming again. The Nunc Dimittis or "Song of Simeon" may also be sung (Luke 2:29-32).

BENEDICTION

The service is closed with the benediction. In the benediction, as in the salutation, the minister has the privilege of speaking for Christ, and bestowing Christ's blessing in the name of the Triune God upon the congregation as it goes forth to live out in full the paradigm of Christian life which it has enacted within its liturgy of worship. Insofar as the minister speaks on behalf of Christ and gives Christ's blessing to the congregation, it is appropriate that canonical words of benediction be used.

The Word in the Sacrament of Baptism

The Sacrament of Baptism will generally be placed either before or after the sermon as a means of grace, a visible word of God. The preferred position of the 1968 *Liturgy and Psalms* was after the offering and doxology as a response to the Word. This sacrament may be placed at the beginning of the serivce insofar as baptism represents cleansing from sin, ingrafting into Christ, and therefore entry into the church.

Because the acknowledgement of corporate sin, as well as of God's forgiveness in Christ, is included in all of the forms for baptism, the sacrament can be used instead of the usual Prayer of Confession, Kyrie, Words of Assurance, and Law.

The *Book of Church Order* of the Reformed Church in America requires that all services of baptism be performed as a part of congregational worship. At least one parent shall be a communicant member of the congregation in which the baptism is taking place, and while "godparents" may be present, it is required that the parents or legal guardians of the child take the vows.

Baptism shall be administered using water by sprinkling, pouring, or immersion in the presence of the entire congregation.

MEANING OF THE SACRAMENT

Baptism is the visible Word of God that we are cleansed in Christ's blood, buried with him into death that we might rise with him and walk in newness of life. In baptism we participate in the covenant of salvation, are ingrafted into the Body of Christ, and are sealed by the sanctifying power of the Holy Spirit.

INSTITUTION

The dominical words of Matthew 28:18-20 should be used.

VOWS

The Christian names of the persons to be baptized shall be used, and in case of infant baptism parents or legal guardians shall respond to the questions.

The members of the congregation are also asked to make vows accepting responsibility for the nurture and upbringing of the baptized, and together will confess their faith in the words of the Nicene or Apostles' Creed.

PRAYER

A prayer will be offered to God in thanksgiving for the grace shown through Jesus Christ and signed and sealed by this baptism.

ADMINISTRATION OF THE SACRAMENT

Christian names (to the exclusion of family names) are used as the person/s are baptized in the Triune name.

The requirement of the state for the naming of the child at birth, coupled with the frequent delay of several weeks for the baptism of the child, have obscured the ancient Christian custom of giving the child its name at baptism. The family name is part of the child's inheritance by birth, but the "Christian name" is given at baptism, marking him or her as a Christian. The church should not further confuse the issue by using family names at the baptismal service.

If baptism is to be performed by sprinkling, the nature of the sacrament as sign, or "visible word," should be respected, and a generous amount of water should be used in the trine gesture.

Section IV:
A LITURGICAL MISCELLANY

POSITION OF THE MINISTER

Calvin began his service from behind the Lord's Table, signifying that we could approach God only through his Son, Jesus Christ. Only during the service of the Word when the Scriptures were to be read and proclaimed would Calvin ascend the pulpit. After the proclamation he returned to the Table for the service of Response.

In more recent times it has also been suggested that there is a certain appropriateness in beginning the Approach to God at the Baptismal Font, signifying that only as we are baptized into Christ and have been washed in his blood are we able to receive the absolution he promises. For the Service of Grace, the proclamation of the Word could then be done from the pulpit, while the sacrament of the Lord's Supper would be conducted from the Table. Following that same logical sequence, the minister could perhaps best lead the Response from the very midst of the congregation.

CHOIR

As skilled persons of articulate voice and accurate note, the choir is invaluable in leadership in public worship. The choir should always be prepared to assist the congregation in the singing of its hymns and responses, and should be prepared to set the tone desired by minister and choral director. Similarly, the choir can be invaluable in assisting the congregation in clear, articulate spoken responses throughout the service.

When the choir leads in worship through an anthem, that anthem should be a part of the ongoing flow and sequence of the service and not an inserted bit of special music.

The use of the lectionary can be of great assistance to minister, organist, and choir director alike in enabling everyone to know well in advance which Scriptures will be used so that appropriate music can be selected to enhance the service.

The choir and organ should be placed in such a way as to offer maximum support for congregational hymnody, while at the same time minimizing any visual distraction from the means of grace as celebrated at pulpit, font, and table.

LECTIONS AND VARIETY THROUGHOUT THE SERVICE

The use of the lectionary offers a controlling principle for including a disciplined variety within many of the variable elements of the worship service. For example, the passage from the Psalm assigned in the lectionary can be searched for passages appropriate to sentences. The salutation can well come from the Epistle. The hymn of praise may be sought out in terms of the index of scriptural allusions in our hymnals. It is also possible that the lections for the day may contain suggestive material which can be paraphrased for a Prayer of Confession, or that there may be words appropriate to the Words of Assurance (forgiveness). Similarly, the lections may contain material appropriate for the law. The possible use of the Psalm or the Psalter or a sung version of the Psalm is also obvious. During the exegesis of the lections and the preparation of the sermon, consideration should also be given to which confession of faith would be most appropriate—including stanzas from *Our Song of Hope*. Finally, the benediction could also be used from the Epistle from which the lesson is taken.

VIRTUES OF REPETITION

Because much of worship is repetitive, we tend to hear most frequently from those who wish more variety in worship. We tend to overlook the fact that many people cherish the virtues of repetition and will greet unwarranted variety with considerable hostility.

For example, while a wide variety of Scripture can be used for a guide to gratitude at the place where the law is read, the wise pastor will frequently include the Ten Commandments and the Summary of the Law. Similarly, while one will not wish to ignore the treasures of the Heidelberg Catechism, or the pertinent contemporaneity of *Our Song of Hope*, the wise pastor will frequently include the Apostles' Creed for the congregation's confession of faith.

In the same way, while specially written prayers of confession may in many instances be very appropriate, variety should be introduced only when it contributes to an articulation of an element of worship within a coherent structure and flow, and is understood by the congregation. It must never be forgotten that the structured repetition of the liturgy is an important factor in the nurture of God's people.

THEOLOGY OF ANNOUNCEMENTS

Those responsible for the leadership of worship should do all they can to assist the congregation in a knowledgeable awareness of the movement of worship from the votum to the benediction. To accept this responsibility raises anew the necessity for a liturgical theology of announcements.

There are two categories of congregational information which can be placed within the context of the flow of worship. One consists of those occurrences within the life of the church where the members are called upon to offer themselves in service. Such announcements could well be made as a part of the offertory. Theologically and liturgically, this would have the advantage of verifying the nature of the event.

A second category consists of announcements of births, weddings, healings, and other occasions for thanksgiving, as well as announcements which seek the prayers and sympathy of the congregation for those who have suffered loss through illness, death, or other distress. Most appropriately, these announcements should be made immediately prior to the prayers of thanksgiving and intercession in which these persons are to be remembered.

In sum, a proper liturgical theology would divide announcements into three groupings: the intercessory, which are made immediately prior to the intercessory prayer; those seeking the offering of self in service, which are made as part of the offertory; and all others which are made before or after the service or are preferably confined to the church bulletin.

RESPECTING THE CONGREGATION

Ministers frequently fall into the habit of demeaning the congregation through excessive verbal instruction. For example, when there is a printed bulletin, there is no need to announce the hymn. It is good to allow the organist to play through the hymn once so that newcomers may become familiar with the tune. The congregation does not need to be told when to stand or when to sit. A simple gesture, or better the example of the minister and choir will be adequate. Verbal instructions are breaks in the flow of the service and create an unnaturalness that is not necessary. The minister does not serve as a master of ceremonies but as a servant of the liturgy, which is the service of the people in the worship of God.

When the structure and flow of worship have been given due consideration by the worship leadership of the church, there will be an eager expectation on the part of the congregation that will enable the service to flow smoothly as a dialogue between leader and congregation in praise of Almighty God.

PART V

Our Song
of Hope

OUR SONG OF HOPE

Our Song of Hope may be used as a Confession of Faith (General Synod, 1978). The opening declaration may be said or sung (Rejoice in the Lord, 610) after which the worship leader declares the title of the section (e.g., "Our Hope in the Coming of the Lord"), to which the congregation responds with the selected stanza/s (e.g., "We are a people of hope..."), followed by the concluding prayer, which may also be sung.

We sing to our Lord a new song;
We sing in our world a sure Hope:
  Our God loves this world,
    God called it into being,
    God renews it through Jesus Christ,
    God governs it by the Spirit.
God is the world's true Hope.

I.   Our Hope in the Coming of the Lord

1.   We are a people of hope
      waiting for the return of our Lord.
  God has come to us
      through the ancient people of Israel,
      as the true Son of God, Jesus of Nazareth,
      as the Holy Spirit at work in our world.
  Our Lord speaks to us now through the inspired Scriptures.
    Christ is with us day by day.

II.   Our Song in a Hopeless World

2.   We know Christ to be our only hope.
    We have enmeshed our world in a realm of sin,
      rebelled against God,
      accepted inhuman oppression of humanity,
      and even crucified God's son.
    God's world has been trapped by our fall,
      governments entangled by human pride,
      and nature polluted by human greed.

III.   Jesus Christ our only Hope

3.   Our only hope is Jesus Christ.
       After we refused to live in the image of God,
       He was born of the virgin Mary,
           sharing our genes and our instincts,
           entering our culture, speaking our language,
           fulfilling the law of our God.
       Being united to Christ's humanity,
           we know ourselves when we rest in Him.

4.   Jesus Christ is the hope of God's world.
       In His death,
           the justice of God is established;
           forgiveness of sin is proclaimed.
       On the day of the resurrection,
           the tomb was empty; His disciples saw Him;
           death was defeated; new life had come.
           God's purpose for the world was sealed.

5.   Our ascended Lord gives hope for two ages.
       In the age to come, Christ is the judge,
           rejecting unrighteousness,
           isolating God's enemies to hell,
           blessing the new creation in Christ.
       In this age, the Holy Spirit is with us,
           calling nations to follow God's path,
           uniting people through Christ in love.

IV.   Our Hope in God's Words

6.   The Holy Spirit speaks through the Scriptures.
    The Spirit has inspired Hebrew and Greek words,
        setting God's truth in human language,
        placing God's teaching in ancient cultures,
        proclaiming the Gospel in the history of the world.
    The Spirit speaks truly what the nations must know,
        translating God's word into modern languages,
        impressing it on human hearts and cultures.

7.   The Holy Spirit speaks through the Church,
        measuring its words by the canonical Scriptures.
    The Spirit has spoken in the ancient creeds,
        and in the confessions of the Reformation.
    The world is called to bear witness to Christ
        in faithfulness to the Scriptures,
        in harmony with the church of the ages,
        and in unity with all Christ's people.

8.   God's Spirit speaks in the world
        according to God's ultimate word in Christ.
    In every time and place,
        in ancient cities and distant lands,
        in technology and business,
        in art and education,
    God has not been left without a witness.
    The Word has entered where we have failed to go.

9.   In each year and in every place
        we expect the coming of Christ's Spirit.
    As we listen to the world's concerns,
        hear the cry of the oppressed,
        and learn of new discoveries,
    God will give us knowledge,
        teach us to respond with maturity,
        and give us courage to act with integrity.

V. Our Hope in Daily Life

10. As citizens we acknowledge the Spirit's work in human
government
    for the welfare of the people,
    for justice among the poor,
    for mercy towards the prisoner,
    against inhuman oppression of humanity.
We must obey God above all rulers,
    waiting upon the Spirit,
    filled with the patience of Christ.

11. We pray for the fruits of the Spirit of Christ
    who works for peace on earth,
    commands us to love our enemies,
    and calls for patience among the nations.
We give thanks for God's work among governments,
    seeking to resolve disputes by means other than war,
    placing human kindness above national pride,
    replacing the curse of war with international self-control.

12. We hear the Spirit's call to love one another
opposing discrimination of race or sex,
inviting us to accept one another,
and to share at every level
    in work and play,
    in church and state,
    in marriage and family,
and so fulfill the love of Christ.

13. As male and female we look to the Spirit
Who makes us the stewards of life
    to plan its beginning,
    to love in its living,
    and to care in its dying.
God makes us the stewards of marriage
    with its lifelong commitment to love;
    yet God knows our frailty of heart.

14. The Spirit leads us into Truth—
the Truth of Christ's salvation,
into increasing knowledge of all existence.
    He rejoices in human awareness of God's creation
    and gives freedom to those on the frontiers of research.
We are overwhelmed by the growth in our knowledge.
    While our truths come in broken fragments,
    we expect the Spirit to unite these in Christ.

VI. Our Hope in the Church

15. Christ elects the church
    to proclaim the Word and celebrate the sacraments,
    to worship God's name,
    and to live as true disciples.
He creates a community
    to be a place of prayer,
    to provide rest for the weary,
    and to lead people to share in service.

16. The Holy Spirit sends the church
to call sinners to repentance,
to proclaim the good news
    that Jesus is personal Savior and Lord.
The Spirit sends it out in ministry
    to preach good news to the poor,
    righteousness to the nations,
    and peace among all people.

17. The Holy Spirit builds one church,
    united in one Lord and one hope,
    with one ministry around one table.
The Spirit calls all believers in Jesus
    to respond in worship together,
    to accept all the gifts from the Spirit,
    to learn from each other's traditions,
    to make unity visible on earth.

18. Christ places baptism in the world
as a seal of God's covenant people,
    placing them in ministry,
    assuring them of the forgiveness of sins.
God knows those who are baptized in Jesus' name,
    guiding the church gently to lead us,
    calling us back when we go astray,
    promising life amid trials and death.

19. Christ places the Lord's table in this world.
Jesus takes up our bread and wine
    to represent His sacrifice,
    to bind His ministry to our daily work,
    to unite us in His righteousness.
Here Christ is present in His world
    proclaiming salvation until He comes,
    a symbol of hope for a troubled age.

VII. Our Hope in the Age to Come

20.   God saves the world through Jesus.
     Those who call on that name will have life.
   Christ's hand reaches out beyond those who say "Lord"
     to the infants who live in the atmosphere of faith,
     even to the farthest stars and planets—all creation.
   The boundaries of God's love are not known,
     the Spirit works at the ends of the world
     before the church has there spoken a word.

21.   God will renew the world through Jesus,
   who will put all unrighteousness out,
     purify the works of human hands,
     and perfect their fellowship in divine love.
   Christ will wipe away every tear;
     death shall be no more.
   There will be a new heaven and a new earth,
     and all creation will be filled with God's glory.

OUR PRAYER:

   Come, Lord Jesus:
     We are open to your Spirit.
     We await your full presence.
     Our world finds rest in you alone.